Springer Series in Language and Communication 9

Editor: W. J. M. Levelt

Springer Series in Language and Communication
Editor: W. J. M. Levelt

Volume 1 **Developing Grammars**
By W. Klein and N. Dittmar

Volume 2 **The Child's Conception of Language** 2nd Printing
Editors: A. Sinclair, R. J. Jarvella, and W. J. M. Levelt

Volume 3 **The Logic of Language Development in Early Childhood**
By M. Miller

Volume 4 **Inferring from Language**
By L. G. M. Noordman

Volume 5 **Retrieval from Semantic Memory**
By W. Noordman-Vonk

Volume 6 **Semantics from Different Points of View**
Editors: R. Bäuerle, U. Egli, A. von Stechow

Volume 7 **Lectures on Language Performance**
By Ch. E. Osgood

Volume 8 **Speech Act Classification**
By Th. Ballmer and W. Brennenstuhl

Volume 9 **The Development of Metalinguistic Abilities in Children**
By D. T. Hakes

David T. Hakes

The Development of Metalinguistic Abilities in Children

In Collaboration with
Judith S. Evans and William Tunmer

With 6 Figures

Springer-Verlag Berlin Heidelberg New York 1980

Professor Dr. David T. Hakes

University of Texas at Austin, Department of Psychology
Austin, TX 78712, USA

Series Editor:

Professor Dr. Willem J. M. Levelt

Max-Planck-Institut für Psycholinguistic, Berg en Dalseweg 79
6522 BC Nijmegen, The Netherlands

ISBN 3-540-10295-7 Springer-Verlag Berlin Heidelberg New York
ISBN 0-387-10295-7 Springer-Verlag New York Heidelberg Berlin

Library of Congress Cataloging in Publication Data, Hakes, David T. 1934- The development of metalinguistic abilities in children. (Springer series in language and communication; v. 9). Bibliography: p. Includes index. 1. Language acquisition. 2. Language awareness. 3. Cognition in children. I. Title. II. Series. P118.H28 401′.9 80-24089 ISBN 0-387-10295-7 (U.S.)

Offset printing and bookbinding: Brühlsche Universitätsdruckerei, Giessen
2153/3130-543210

Preface

Not very many years ago, it was common for language researchers and theorists to argue that language development was somehow special and separate from other aspects of development. It was a period when the "little linguist" view of language development was common, and much discussion was devoted to developmental "linguistic universals," in contrast to more broadly defined cognitive universals.

It seemed to me at the time (and still does) that such views reflected more their promulgators' ignorance of those aspects of cognitive development most likely to provide illuminating parallels with language development than they did the true developmental state of affairs. Coming from a neo-Piagetian frame of reference, it seemed to me that there were striking parallels between the development of children's language comprehension abilities and the cognitive developmental changes occurring contemporaneously, largely during the period Piaget characterized as the preoperational stage. And, though more difficult to see even now, there appeared also to be developmentally earlier parallels during the sensory-motor stage.

But having thought through the problem of parallels that far, I then hit a barrier. Whether one subscribes to the Piagetian ontogeny or not, it is clear that middle childhood is a time marked by major cognitive developmental changes, among them the changes Piaget characterized as the onset of concrete operations. But in language development there was not an immediately obvious homologous change. In both language comprehension and language production it seemed that middle childhood was a period of refinement of performances whose initiation had begun considerably earlier.

Does the parallel really break down in middle childhood? Might it really be the case that all of the abilities required for dealing with language were ones that were already available to the preoperational child and that what continued to develop was simply the variety of content the child could talk about and understand? If so, this would make language different from other aspects of cognition, but not at all in the way envisioned by those who argued that it was special.

At long last, it occurred to me that I was looking in the wrong place for linguistic parallels to cognitive development in middle childhood. Much of the emphasis in the cognitive developmental literature is on how older and younger children perform differently *on the same tasks*. In studying the development of conservation, for example, the tasks used with younger and older children remain the same. What changes is the children's judgments and explanations.

What this emphasis on within-task changes obscures is the fact that the developmental changes also involve children becoming able to deal with *a greater variety of tasks*. They become able to behave systematically and effectively in a variety of situations in which, when younger, they had no systematic (or effective) behaviors.

Might it be that this was what characterized linguistic development in middle childhood - that children became able to do a greater variety of things with language than just understand and produce it? If so, what might these things be? It was then that I was reminded of what Chomsky had been pointing out for some years - that the competent speaker-hearer of a language not only produces and understands it but, in addition, has intuitions about it. Might it be the emergence of such linguistic intuitions that provided the missing parallel to cognitive developmental changes in middle childhood?

At the time I was first thinking all of this through, there was very little research available on children's linguistic intuitions, for this was contemporaneous with Courtney Cazden's coining of the term "metalinguistic abilities" to refer to the abilities underlying these intuitions. It was then that the outlines of the research presented here first began to be formulated. Since that time there has, of course, been virtually an explosion of interest in and research on children's developing metalinguistic abilities. In the past few years we have had our consciousness of children's consciousness of language raised considerably. But even now there are still few attempts, either empirical or conceptual, to link different metalingustic abilities to each other or to other aspects of cognitive delvopment. I hope that the research and discussion presented here will provide a few small beginnings toward uncovering those relationships and will stimulate others to think about and explore how the pieces of the puzzle fit together.

A great many individuals and organizations contributed in a variety of ways to this project, and their assistance is gratefully acknowledged. My collaborators, Judy Evans and Bill Tunmer, contributed endless hours of cajoling the children into contributing their data and also contributed numerous ideas. The research itself would not have been possible without the generous support of The Grant Foundation, Inc., and the National Institute of Child Health and Human Development, or without the cooperation of the teachers of the Child Craft Schools, the Trinity Lutheran Child Care Center, and the Highland Park Elementary School, all in Austin, Texas. And to the children who consented to play our silly games I owe a deep debt. There are, in addition, numerous other, including several anonymous reviewers, whose contributions are acknowledged with gratitude. There is, finally, a deep intellectual debt owed to Tom Bever, for it was, in the beginning, numerous long and probing discussions with Tom that first stimulated me to think about this problem and to think about it in the ways I have.

Austin, Texas   David T. Hakes
March, 1980

Contents

Chapter 1 Introduction 1

1.1 Recent Trends in Research on Linguistic Development 2
1.2 Relationships Between Linguistic and Cognitive Development 4
    1.2.1 The Sensory-Motor Period 4
    1.2.2 The Preoperational Period 5
    1.2.3 The Transition from Preoperations to Concrete Operations ... 14

Chapter 2 The Nature and Development of Metalinguistic Abilities 21

2.1 The Development of Metalinguistic Abilities 24
2.2 Relationships Between Metalinguistic and Cognitive Developments ... 35

Chapter 3 A Study of Children's Metalinguistic Abilities: Method 41

3.1 Tasks and Materials 42
    3.1.1 Conservation 42
    3.1.2 Synonymy 42
        Active, Passive, and Cleft Sentences 43
        Locative Existential Sentences 44
        Temporal Relations Sentences 45
        Spatial Relations Sentences 46
        Size and Amount Sentences 47
        The Synonymy Task 48
    3.1.3 Comprehension 48
        The Comprehension Task 49
    3.1.4 Acceptability 50
        Word-Order Changes 52
        Violations of Strict Subcategorization Rules 53
        Violations of Selectional Restrictions 53

Indeterminates, Indefinites, and Negation 54

Inalienable Possession 55

Meaningful False Sentences 55

The Acceptability Task 56

3.1.5 Phonemic Segmentation 57

3.2 Subjects 57

3.3 Procedure 58

Chapter 4   A Study of Children's Metalinguistic Abilities: Results and
Discussion 61

4.1 Conservation 61

4.2 Comprehension 63

4.3 Synonymy 65

4.4 Acceptability 73

4.5 Segmentation 88

4.6 Relationships Among the Tasks 90

Chapter 5   Reflections on Reflecting on Language 97

References 109

Subject Index 117

Chapter 1   Introduction

"Mommy, get it ladder." Most adult speakers of English have little difficulty understanding utterances such as this one, produced by a 2½-year-old. Yet most would also agree that there is something wrong with the utterance, that it is not a well-formed sentence of English. As linguists have been pointing out for some time, the knowledge that mature speakers of a language possess permits them not only to produce and understand utterances in that language but, in addition, to reflect upon and evaluate those utterances. This sort of reflection and evaluation has generally been referred to as involving "linguistic intuitions."

Our linguistic intuitions are, of course, not limited to the evaluation of utterances produced by young children. Adult speakers occasionally produce utterances that they themselves realize after the fact were not well formed. And listeners sometimes notice that there is something wrong with the ways in which adult speakers have expressed themselves.

Similarly, it is common for linguists (and others) to point out that speakers of English know that "bench" is an English word but that "bnench" is not. Presumably this results from their knowing that "bn" does not occur as a consonant cluster in English, not because such a sound sequence is unpronounceable. "Blench" causes many English speakers considerably more difficulty: is it an English word or not? The problem arises because of the intuition that it *could* be an English word, that its sequence of phonemes is one that is possible in English. The uncertainty is over whether it is merely a possible word or is an actual one (see FOSS and HAKES 1978). (In fact, "blench" is an English word, albeit a rare one, meaning essentially "to turn pale.")

Although such intuitions do not often intrude themselves into our everyday understanding and producing of language, their existence has been a familiar fact for quite some time. Nonetheless it is only relatively recently that the abilities that make such intuitions possible — abilities which, following CAZDEN (1972, 1975), will be referred to here as "metalinguistic" abilities — have begun to be explored. More to the point, it is also only recently that systematic attention has begun being paid to questions about when and how such metalinguistic abilities arise in children in the course of their acquiring language. For example, do the abilities that involve reflecting upon language arise as automatic consequences of learning to produce and understand utterances? When children acquire the ability to understand passive sentences (e.g., "The clown was kissed by the girl."), do they automatically also recognize that these are synonymous with active sentences (e.g., "The girl kissed the clown.")?

The main concern here is with the question of when and how metalinguistic abilities emerge in children. The hypothesis proposed here is that metalinguistic abilities are different from, and emerge later than, the abilities involved in producing and understanding language. Specifically, it is proposed that metalinguistic abilities show their greatest development during middle childhood, the period between, roughly, 4 and 8 years. Further, it will be argued that their emergence is the linguistic manifestation of the cognitive developmental changes which Piaget has characterized as the emergence of concrete operational thought.

The purpose of this book is to explore the development of children's metalinguistic abilities, both empirically and conceptually, and to provide some tentative suggestions about the underlying nature of metalinguistic development. In doing so, some of the currently available data and theorizing on linguistic and cognitive development and the possible relations among these developments will be considered first. Then, the research on metalinguistic development that was the occasion for all of these ruminations will be presented. And finally, the implications of this research and of other work on metalinguistic development for a theory of linguistic and cognitive development will be considered.

1.1 Recent Trends in Research on Linguistic Development

Since the early 1960s, research and theorizing about linguistic development in children have been accruing at a rapidly increasing rate. The 1960s might well be regarded as the decade of child syntax, for the primary focus of research and theorizing was the development of the structure of children's utterances. Interest in this topic was stimulated both by far-reaching developments in linguistic theory and by the pioneering studies of what FERGUSON and SLOBIN (1973) have termed "the Harvard children," "the Berkeley children," and "the Maryland children." The bulk of the work during this period focused on children's utterances in the age range bounded at the lower end by an age soon after that at which children begin producing utterances with overt structure (roughly, 18-24 months), and at the upper end by an age of 4 or 5 years, an age by which some early researchers suggested the structure of children's utterances was approaching that of adults'.

More recently, the concerns of language development researchers have broadened considerably. Increasing attention is being paid to linguistic developments in the age period preceding overtly structured utterances. Interest in the semantic and pragmatic aspects of linguistic development has also increased considerably, stimulated both by the increased importance accorded these topics by linguists and by such counterintuitive findings as those of DONALDSON and BALFOUR (1968) on children's developing comprehension of the meanings of "more" and "less." Increased attention has also been focused on the development of children's language comprehension abilities.

In general, however, attention has continued to be focused primarily on developments occurring before the age of 5 years, with considerably less attention being accorded to linguistic development during middle childhood. Equally important, most studies of linguistic development during middle childhood have focused on relatively isolated phenomena, such as the developing comprehension of one or a small group of related sentence types or the development of the meanings of a few closely related words. Consequently, our knowledge of linguistic development, and particularly of *patterns* of linguistic development, during this period is rather less than for earlier age periods.

It has also become increasingly common in recent years for language development researchers to explore (or at least consider) how linguistic development might be related to other aspects of cognitive development. Again, the bulk of this work has focused on linguistic-cognitive developmental relationships in early childhood, with particular emphasis on the period prior to 2 years of age. Relatively little attention has been paid to possible linguistic-cognitive developmental relationships during either what the Piagetians refer to as the preoperational period or the period of the transition from preoperational to concrete operational functioning.

The aim here is to extend this discussion, focusing on relationships between linguistic and cognitive developments during the preoperational period and, particularly, during the transition from this period to the concrete operational period.

1.2 Relationships Between Linguistic and Cognitive Development

General discussions of the nature of relationships between linguistic and
cognitive development across the entirety of development have been infrequent.
Piaget's view that cognitive development precedes and lays the foundation for
linguistic development is, of course, well known (see SINCLAIR 1969, 1975,
1978). And BATES et al. (1977) have discussed the variety of logically possible relationships (see also MOERK 1975). But the most extensive discussions
have focused on developments during the sensory-motor period, the period during which children first begin using language productively.

1.2.1 The Sensory-Motor Period

BRUNER (1975, 1977) has argued that the transition from prelinguistic to linguistic interactions between infants and adults arises as a consequence of
changes in the nature of infant-adult social interactions. To the extent that
the requisite social interactions are themselves contingent for their development upon perceptual and cognitive developments on the infant's part, the
argument is essentially that linguistic communication does not begin until
several prerequisite perceptual, cognitive, and social developments have occurred. FLAVELL (1977) and TREVARTHEN (1977), among others, have suggested
some of the developments that may be relevant.

BATES et al. (1975) have also suggested the existence of a cognitive-linguistic developmental link during the sensory-motor period. On the basis of
longitudinal data from a small number of children, they argued that several
pragmatic functions of language are served linguistically only after they
have first appeared in nonlinguistic forms. These developments are, they suggest, consequences of the attainment of Stages V and VI of Piaget's ontogeny
of sensory-motor development (see also BATES et al. 1977; DORE 1974, 1975).
GREENFIELD and SMITH (1976) have considered some of the possible cognitive
underpinnings of the meanings which they see children's early one-word utterances as expressing. And BROWN (1973) and EDWARDS (1973) have discussed
some possible sensory-motor cognitive antecedents of the meanings expressed
by children's early multiple-word utterances, that is, at Brown's Stage I.

If there is any consensus among these and other researchers regarding the
kind of relationship that obtains between cognitive and linguistic developments during the sensory-motor period, it is that a particular kind of cognitive achievement is prerequisite for some related kind of linguitics development. That is, the former is a necessary, but not sufficient, condition for
the latter. MACNAMARA (1972, 1977) has stated this view explicitly, and it is

certainly implicity in BROWN's (1973) questioning of where the meanings of
the earliest multiple-word utterances might come from if they did not come
from the sensory-motor achievements that immediately precede them.

As yet, the data do not allow a detailed account of the nature of the relationships between particular cognitive and particular linguistic developments during this period. And, as CORRIGAN (1979) suggests, it seems likely
that the relationships are more complex than anticipated by most current discussions. But meager as our knowledge is of the relationships during this
period, there are even fewer explicit discussions of or suggestions about the
nature of cognitive-linguistic relationships during subsequent developmental
periods.

1.2.2 The Preoperational Period

The transition from sensory-motor to preoperational cognitive functioning is
generally regarded as occurring during the last half of the child's second
year. It is, of course, roughly contemporaneous with this transition that
children begin producing multiple-word utterances in some profusion, and it
seems highly unlikely that this temporal coincidence is only coincidental.
But how these developmental milestones might be related is less than clear.
As noted earlier, BROWN (1973) and EDWARDS (1973) have pointed to antecedent,
sensory-motor cognitive achievements as the bases of the meanings expressed
by these early structured utterances. And it seems likely that Piaget's characterization of this transition as involving the emergence of symbolic representation is one that has significance for the linguistic developments accompanying the transition. Perhaps the structured utterances that emerge early
in the preoperational period encode information differently than their one-
word predecessors, that is, they stand in a different kind of relationship to
the situations they are about. But clearly, much remains to be discovered.

The nature of cognitive-linguistic developmental relationships *during* the
preoperational period is fully as problematic. Although this period is the
one for which we have the richest data of any period of linguistic development, it is also a period which, until quite recently, has received relatively
little attention from cognitive developmental researchers and theorists. It
is, rather, the end of the preoperational period and the transition from this
to the subsequent concrete operational period that have been the focus of
both empirical and conceptual attention. And the result of this emphasis is
that we have, as yet, relatively little insight into the nature of cognitive
developments and functioning during this preoperational period.

As has often been remarked, the typical characterization of preoperational children focuses on all the things which their older, concrete operational counterparts can do but which they can't do, leaving the impression that they are extremely incompetent. This impression, misleading though it is, may be one of the sources of the view, commonly expounded during the 1960s and early 1970s, that language develops separately and apart from other aspects of cognition. It is clear that great strides in language development are made during the preoperational period. If, during the same period, there are not comparably great advances elsewhere, then language must be following a developmental course of its own.

But the impression that the preoperational period is one of cognitive stagnation and lack of achievement is a misleading one, resulting more from inattention by researchers than from the preoperational children's cognitive capabilities themselves. One reason for this situation is undoubtedly methodological: 2- and 3-year-olds are not the most tractable of experimental subjects. Research techniques useable with infants and younger children, ones that characteristically do not depend upon very active cooperation from the subjects, are no longer useable with the active, mobile children of the late sensory-motor and early preoperational periods. And the active cooperation necessary for applying techniques useable with older children is obtainable, at best, only for very short periods and in small amounts from these children.

There is, in addition, another reason that the cognitive accomplishments of the preoperational period are likely to be underestimated: many of them are of sorts that can be characterized as involving "'mundane cognition,' or the cognitive behavior of everyday life" (FLAVELL 1977, p.78). As such, they are accomplishments whose nature and significance are not readily noticed, even though they may play important roles in children's changing and expanding interactions with the social and physical worlds.

Despite the paucity of data and theorizing concerning cognitive development during the preoperational period, it appears that there do exist significant parallels between the linguistic and cognitive accomplishments of this period. In seeking such parallels, it seems reasonable to suppose that children's linguistic accomplishments during this period should have the same characteristics as their cognitive counterparts: they too should be changes in the ways in which children deal with the mundane, everyday world. This certainly seems to be the case for their language production capabilities, for they are gradually becoming capable of producing better-formed utterances about a gradually expanding variety of subject matters.

Language production does not, however, seem the best place to seek linguistic-cognitive parallels, if only because so little is known about the
production of other kinds of behaviors and, particularly, about the developmental changes in the mechanisms underlying such behaviors. Since our scant
knowledge of cognitive developmental changes in this period is greatest concerning the ways in which children perceive and understand the world that
impinges upon them, we might expect to find the clearest evidence of linguistic parallels in the ways preoperational children perceive and understand
the linguistic inputs that impinge upon them. Thus, it is to the development
of children's language comprehension abilities that we should look for the
parallels.

One notable characteristic of the development of language comprehension
during this period is that it does not always proceed smoothly, children pro-
gressing gradually from noncomprehension to comprehension. Rather, it is
marked by considerable irregularity, comprehension often become worse before
it becomes better. Evidence of this was provided by BEVER (1970), who presented children between 2 and 6 years with reversible active and passive
sentences like (1.1) and (1.2),

The cow kisses the horse.   (1.1)
The horse is kissed by the cow.   (1.2)

asking the children to act out the sentences with toys. The youngest children
performed near chance for both types of sentences, sometimes makings the toy
cow "kiss" the toy horse, and sometimes the reverse. Performance on the active
sentences improved steadily with increasing age, so that by 5 years the children performed nearly perfectly. Performance on the passives, however, did
not improve in any straightforward way with increasing age. Rather, it first
declined to a level worse than chance, and only later improved to a better-
than-chance level. Between 3 and 4 years, the children were more likely to
make the toy horse kiss the toy cow for sentence (1.2) than the reverse. Subsequently, performance improved steadily, so that the 5- and 6-year-olds performed nearly as well on passives as on actives. Similar results have since
been obtained in several other studies (see CHAPMAN and KOHN 1977 for a brief
review).

This pattern of worsening comprehension followed by improvement is not
unique to passive sentences. BEVER (1970), for example, has found that comprehension of reversible object-cleft sentences like (1.3) parallels that of

passives in its development, while comprehension of reversible subject-cleft sentences like (1.4) parallels the developmental course of actives.

It is the horse that the cow kisses.   (1.3)
It is the cow that kisses the horse.   (1.4)

These results, and others like them, suggest that, at the beginning of the preoperational period, children have not yet begun to attend to or taken account of the information conveyed by a sentence's word order. Hence, their performance on reversible sentences, ones in which word order information is important, is essentially random. At the same time, however, children perform at a level considerably better than chance on sentences whose interpretations are uniquely determined by the meanings of their content words alone. This suggests that, initially, children's comprehension of sentences is based entirely upon their understanding of the meanings of the sentences' content words (see BEVER 1970; GOWIE and POWERS 1978; SINCLAIR and BRONCKART 1972). Where there is only one way in which a sentence's words can be put together, disregarding order, that makes sense in terms of the child's knowledge of the words' meanings and of the world, then the child "understands" it. But where word order is crucial to deciding between two or more otherwise plausible meanings, performance is essentially random.

The comprehension performance of 3-year-olds suggests that they have begun to take account of a sentence's word order, but also that they interpret word order in an invariant way. That is, the order Noun-Verb-Noun (NVN) is interpreted as indicating a Subject-Verb-Object (SVO) grammatical structure, one in which the first-occurring noun is the subject of the action labelled by the verb. (For present purposes it is immaterial whether the structure is a syntactic one — Subject-Verb-Object — or a semantic one — Agent-Action-Patient.) Such an interpretive rule allows these children to interpret active and subject-cleft sentences correctly; for both, the rule NVN→SVO yields the correct interpretation. But applying the same rule to either passives or object clefts yields incorrect interpretations as systematically as it does correct interpretations for actives and subject clefts.

Thus, one element in children's changing comprehension performance between 3 and 4 years is the development of attention to a sentence's word order and use of that, in addition to the words' meanings, as the basis for inferring the sentence's meaning. Although the NVN→SVO rule is too simple and inflexible to allow children to understand the full variety of sentences they hear, it is a fairly useful rule. NVN sequences occur quite commonly in English, and an NVN sequence is more likely than not to be associated with an SVO structure. The nature of the development appears to be that the child is discovering the existence of a correlation between a characteristic of the superficial, readily available form of sentences and a characteristic of their underlying meaning. This implies both that the child frequently has access to information other than a sentence itself about that sentence's meaning — a point frequently suggested (see, e.g., MACNAMARA 1972, 1977) — and that the child is capable of computing, across occasions, the correlations between sentences' characteristics, even when those correlations are considerably less than perfect.

The 3-year-old's problem is, in a sense, that s/he has not yet discovered that there are properties in addition to a sentence's word meanings and word order that must be taken into account. S/he has not yet discovered the other properties of sentences that signal that they are exceptions to the NVN→SVO rule. As FLAVELL has remarked about similar developmental patterns in other domains, "Sometimes the reward for a child's growing information-processing skills is a temporary conceptual mistake, a mistake he was previously too cognitively immature to make and one he will subsequently correct when he matures still further," (FLAVELL 1977, p.74).

What remains for 3-year-olds to learn in order to understand passives and other sentences for which the NVN→SVO rule does not hold is, first of all, that there are exceptions, that the correlation between the superficial word order and the underlying structure is less than perfect. In addition, they must discover what cues signal the presence of exceptions. For passives, these include the presence (and particular form) of an auxiliary verb, the presence (for most main verbs) of a distinctive suffix, and for full passives the presence of "by" between the main verb and the following noun phrase. And finally, they must discover the appropriate interpretation to associate with each kind of exception.

There are, of course, many other attentional and interpretive rules, or heuristic strategies, for language comprehension developing during the same period (see, e.g., CHAPMAN and KOHN 1977; SLOBIN 1973). Many of these interact with the ones mentioned here; others come into play for interpreting other types of sentences. But in general the development of language comprehension during the preoperational period appears to involve differentiating (i.e., noticing) and attending to properties of sentences that were not noticed or attended to earlier. In addition, it involves developing strategies for interpreting the patterns of properties attended to. At this level of generalization, the course of development appears to be more or less continuous. At the level of particular sentence types, however, the course of development is often discontinuous.

The character of the heuristic strategies developed for language comprehension — interpretative rules that work often but not always — suggests a possible parallel to other developments occurring during the preoperational period. The nature of the parallel is suggested by Piaget's characterization of preoperational thought as "intuitive." It is perhaps most readily evident in the performance of preoperational children on one of the most characteristic of Piagetian tasks — conversation.

Preoperational children do not typically give correct answers when, following the transformation in a conservation task, they are asked about the equality of the arrays. Nor are their explanations like those of older, concrete operational children. What is significant is that older preoperational children give incorrect answers *systematically*; their performance is worse than chance rather than random. In number conservation tasks, for example, in which one array is transformed so as to be longer than the other, they generally judge that the longer row has more. Similarly, in continuous quantity conservation tasks, older preoperational children generally say that the container whose surface level is higher has more. Further, the explanations given for such judgments indicate clearly that the children are attending to and responding on the basis of the perceptual properties of the post-transformational display, properties such as length, height, etc. (see, e.g., SMITHER et al. 1974).

Although younger preoperational children (i.e., 2- and 3-year-olds) have been tested less often and with a lesser variety of conservation tasks, it appears that their performance is different from that of older preoperational children and still older concrete operational children. Rather than consistently making either correct or incorrect judgments, they perform at chance or, in some cases, slightly better than chance (see, e.g., BEVER et al. 1968; LAPOINTE and O'DONNELL 1974; PUFALL and SHAW 1972).

Thus, the developmental course of conservation task performance during the preoperational period parallels that on many language comprehension tasks: it is initially neither very good nor very bad; with increasing age it worsens; and eventually it improves, with the onset of concrete operations, to become consistently good. Further, it appears that the nature of the developments underlying these changes is also similar in kind to that underlying the changes in language comprehension performance.

The fact that older preoperational children respond consistently in conservation tasks on the basis of properties such as length and height indicates that they are attending to such properties as isolable characteristics of the objects and situations in which they occur. In addition, the consistency of their performance suggests that they have developed heuristic strategies for making inferences on the basis of such properties. As in the language comprehension case, they appear to be using relatively superficial, easy-to-compute properties of the displays as bases for inferring other, more difficult to evaluate properties, such as number from length and volume from height. The properties inferred and the properties from which they are inferred are different in the conservation and comprehension cases, but both appear to involve the same kind of inferential process.

The inferential rules-of-thumb used in conservation tasks, like their counterparts in language comprehension, have considerable ecological validity. Considering the variety of situations likely to be encountered by the preoperational child (or by an adult, for that matter), the properties inferred are ones that are correlated with those from which they are inferred. It is, for example, probably generally true that for two linear arrays of objects, the longer contains the greater number. Thus, a LONGER→MORE rule, like the NVN→SVO rule, works more often than it fails. The shortcoming of such heuristic rules is, of course, that the correlations are less than perfect. The consequence is that if such a rule is applied to a case in which the properties are not correlated, either through lack of knowledge of the exceptions or through misidentifying the case, the inference made will be wrong.

The performance of younger preoperational children in conservation tasks also appears to have a basis similar to that underlying their language comprehension performance. They have, as yet, acquired few of the inferential strategies characteristic of their older preoperational counterparts. In addition, they may not have yet developed the general strategy of attending to isolable properties of situations rather than treating situations as unanalyzed Gestalts. The development of a preference for dealing with situations analytically would appear to be one way of interpreting some of the recent results obtained in studies of the perception of multidimensional stimuli (e.g., KEMLER and SMITH 1978; SHEPP 1978; SMITH and KEMLER 1978). Note that this need not imply that the younger children *cannot* treat situations analytically, only that they characteristically *do not* do so.

The consequence is that, with their as yet meager sets of interpretive strategies, there are not very many situations for which they have bases

available for making consistent inferences, be they correct or incorrect.
The developmental change occurring during the preoperational period is, thus,
the development of attention to isolable superficial properties of situations,
coupled with the acquisition of heuristic strategies for inferring other properties from them. The change is from performing inconsistently to performing
either consistently correctly or consistently incorrectly, depending on whether the situation is one for which the correlation between properties holds
or not. In terms of the strategies developed early, active and subject-cleft
sentences are examples of the former, as are many quantity estimation situations. Passive and object-cleft sentences and conservation tasks are examples
of the latter. It is, by intent, a characteristic of conservation tasks that
in the post-transformation displays the correlations that normally obtain do
not. Consequently, children cannot arrive at correct judgments on the basis
of their inferential strategies. It is, of course, just this property of such
tasks that makes them useful for diagnosing the bases on which children arrive at their judgments.

A particularly clear example of the sort of developmental change we have
been describing concerns children's interpretations of the word "big." MARATSOS
(1973; see also LUMSDEN and POTEAT 1968) asked children to pick the "big" one
from arrays of objects varying in height, width, and area. Three-year-olds
and young 4-year-olds generally chose correctly. But children between 4;6 and
5;11 did not consistently do so. In a later study, MARATSOS (1974a) found
that the older children tended to be influenced strongly by the relative
height of the tops of the objects, that is, to be responding to "big" by selecting the object with the highest top point. They also responded incorrectly
to requests for the "tallest" one when the object with the greatest overall
height did not have have the highest top point.

The developmental change here, like those in the cases discussed earlier,
is in part an increase in the child's tendency to attend to an isolable property of the objects and to use that property as a basis for inferring another,
related property. Maratsos' younger subjects were responding to differences
in the overall area (or volume) of the objects, but without necessarily having analyzed the objects in terms of the dimensions entering into area. That
is, they were dealing with the objects as relatively unanalyzed Gestalts. The
older children, however, give evidence of attending to the dimensional properties of the objects and, in addition, of focusing or "centering" their
attention on a single property of a single dimension. The meaning of "big"
thus changes from being associated with (i.e., inferred from) unanalyzed

global size to being associated with a single property that is sometimes, but not always, correlated with size. Presumably, still later, children become able to attend to multiple dimensions, and the meaning of "big" reverts to global size. (See CLARK 1977 for a similar account of semantic development during the preoperational period.)

The developmental pattern during the preoperational period thus appears to be much the same whether one is considering cognitive development per se, the development of sentence comprehension, or the development of word meaning. The parallel between children's developing linguistic abilities and their developing cognitive abilities arises because the underlying developmental changes are the same. There is, first of all, an increasing tendency to attend to particular superficial properties. This, coupled with the ability to compute correlations between those properties and others, results in the development of heuristic strategies for inferring the presence of some properties from the presence of others. The heuristic character of the preoperational strategies, as well as the fact that their number increases only gradually, gives preoperational children's performance its appearance of inconsistency, the property that led Piaget to characterize it as "intuitive." Thus, a child may perform quite adequately, for example, in a variety of real-world situations in which relative number is predictable from relative length and yet perform consistently incorrectly in number conservation tasks.

It should be noted in passing that it is *not* being suggested that there are straightforward *temporal* correspondences between particular linguistic and cognitive achievements of the preoperational period. There is, for example, no reason to expect that the age at which children are most likely to misinterpret passive sentences should coincide with that at which they err most systematically on number conservation problems. The properties to be inferred are different; the properties they are inferred from are different; and the appropriate heuristic strategies are different. What is the same is the course of the developments, the kinds of things that children are becoming able to do. The fact that the age of worst performance on passive sentences corresponds closely to the age of worse performance on number conservation problems is most probably nothing more than a coincidence.

If the developmental parallel between linguistic development during the preoperational period and cognitive development during the same period is as has been suggested here, we might anticipate that the same sort of relationship would also hold later in the course of development. The period of the transition from preoperational to concrete operational cognitive functioning

is, of course, one about which considerably more is known about the nature
of the cognitive changes occurring than is the case for the preoperational
period per se. Conversely, it is also a period for which considerably less
is known about linguistic developments. Nonetheless, if the parallel holds,
we may expect to gain some insight into the linguistic developments to be
expected by considering the nature of the cognitive developments. If this is
so, how should the linguistic capabilities of 8-year-olds, children at or
near the end of the transition, be different from those of 4-year-olds, children at or approaching the beginning of the transition?

1.2.3 The Transition from Preoperations to Concrete Operations

However one characterizes cognitive development during middle childhood, it
is clear that this is a period during which major changes occur in children's
cognitive functioning. Piaget has argued in numerous places that the thought
of preoperational children tends to be intuitive in the sense suggested earlier, their attention being "centered," or focused, on a single aspect of a
situation at a time. The transition to concrete operations involves, he argued, a progressive increase in the ability to decenter attention. Accompanying this is an increase in the ability to consider multiple aspects of a
situation at the same time, to think about the relationships among them, and
to consider their relationships to aspects of other situations, past or potential, that differ from the immediately present situation.

Whether one accepts the Piagetian characterization of the transition and
of the nature of concrete operational thought itself or not, it seems clear
that some such changes are occurring. In number conservation tasks, for example, there are certainly developmental changes occurring that affect both
children's judgments of the effects of the transformation and their understanding of the reasons why movement does not affect number. Reverting to
Piaget's terminology, an increasing ability to decenter allows the child to
discover the inverse relationship between length and density. More importantly,
it allows the child to consider simultaneously the pre- and post-transformational states of the display. And this, in turn, allows the discovery of the
nature of the relationship between the two and how that relationship is affected (or unaffected, as the case may be) by the transformation. That is,
consideration of the relationships between states allows discovering the differences between operations that change number (i.e., addition and subtraction) and ones that do not (i.e., movement).

Preoperational children have sometimes been characterized as being, relatively speaking, captives of their immediate situations and of the strategies

they have developed for interpreting them, acting on the basis of the interpretations those strategies yield. In a sense, they have no alternative means
for interpreting situations. Concrete operational children, on the other hand,
are becoming increasingly able to deal systematically with relationships,
both between different properties of a situation and between those of the immediate situation and other past or possible situations. And this allows them
to develop alternative means for interpreting situations with which they are
faced, means that in many instances (e.g., conservation and similar tasks)
are more effective than those available earlier.

It should be noted in passing that the development of alternative, concrete operational means for interpreting and responding to situations does
not entail the abandonment of the earlier developed inferential strategies.
These remain, and probably continue to develop, as ways of estimating solutions of problems where exact solutions are not required or not permitted or
where the correlations between surface cues and underlying interpretations
are sufficiently high as to make inferential errors unlikely.

Consider, for example, the way in which we, as adults, decide whether a
particular object is a chair when we are looking for one. Whatever else a
chair may be, it certainly is something of appropriate size, strength, and
shape to support one's weight in a sitting position. That is, an object's
suitability for allowing the "sitting function" is generally the most germane
criterion when one is seeking a chair. But we do not generally approach an
object that might be a chair tentatively, feeling it out and testing it for
strength, stability, and comfort. Rather, we typically look at the object
and, if it appears to have the perceptual qualities that are correlated with
its serving the function of a chair, we attempt to sit on it. Once in a while,
of course, we may be fooled and land soundly (and uncomfortably) on the floor.
But fortunately, the correlation between the visual properties of chairs is
sufficiently high that such painfully incorrect inferences do not occur very
frequently.

But in many cases the correlations are not that high. And for those, concrete operational children, with their increased ability to recognize such
cases and to find alternative ways of dealing with them, are clearly at an
advantage over preoperational children. In this sense, the change is not one
of exchanging one approach for another but, rather, of gaining additional
approaches to perceptual and conceptual problems. It is, that is, an increase
in cognitive flexibility.

A search for linguistic parallels to these cognitive developmental changes
may not, however, be immediately rewarding. Certainly, linguistic development

is far from complete by middle childhood. There can be little doubt that
vocabulary development, both in terms of learning more words and of learning
more about the meanings of known words, continues far past this period. And
certainly the variety of subject matters on which children are able to converse also continues to increase. But it does not appear that there is any
change in the way children approach the tasks of understanding and producing
language that parallels the change in, for example, the way they approach
conservation and similar tasks. Rather, concrete operational children appear
to be doing more of the same kinds of things they were doing earlier, adding
to their comprehension and production abilities, but not changing the ways
they approach these tasks.

To take one example, CAROL CHOMSKY (1969) has found that it is not until
an age certain to fall within or after the transitional period that children
are likely to understand correctly sentences with infinitival complement
constructions embedded under verbs like "ask" and "promise," as in sentences
(1.5) and (1.6)

Michelle asked Judy what to wear to the ballet.   (1.5)
Michael promised David to bring Wendy to the party.   (1.6)

(see also, e.g., CROMER 1970; KESSEL 1970). The reason, CHOMSKY suggested,
is that complement sentences with these main verbs are exceptions to a general rule: it is the noun phrase closest to the complement's infinitive verb
that is that verb's subject. Thus, in sentence (1.7),

Laurie told David to go to the store.   (1.7)

it is David who is to go to the store, while in (1.5) it is what Michelle is
to wear that is in question, and in (1.6) it is Michael who is to bring Wendy
to the party. (The rule of inference is actually rather more complex than
suggested here; see MARATSOS 1974b).

What children must learn in order to understand the "ask" and "promise"
sentences is, first of all, that there are exceptions to this general rule.
In addition, they must learn the surface cues (i.e., the particular verbs)
that signal the presence of exceptions. And finally, they must learn a rule
for interpreting the exceptions. It is not surprising that this should be
difficult and not accomplished until late, if ever (see KRAMER et al. 1972).
There are relatively few sentences that exemplify the general rule and even

fewer that exemplify the exception, and some of the verbs that signal exceptions (e.g., "ask") do so only some of the time.

What is important here, however, is that what children must master in order to understand these exceptional complement sentences has much the same
character as what much younger children must master to understand sentence
constructions such as the passive. They must augment their heuristic interpretive strategies to deal not only with sentences that are consistent with
a general rule but also with the exceptions. And the developmental pattern
of comprehension successes and failures is also similar for the two. For both
there is a period during which some sentences are understood correctly (e.g.,
actives, unexceptional complements) while other, closely related sentences
(e.g., passives, exceptional complements) are systematically misunderstood.

Thus, late developments in language comprehension have much the same character of first acquiring a general interpretive strategy and then acquiring
additional strategies for interpreting the exceptions as their earlier, preoperational counterparts. This implies that these late acquisitions do not
require general cognitive or linguistic abilities that are not already available at the time the earlier strategies are acquired. It appears, then, that
concrete operational children are continuing a kind of development begun earlier, continuing to add to the set of heuristic strategies they have available to bring to bear on understanding sentences and, thus, increasing the
variety of sentences they can understand correctly. But it does not appear
that language comprehension in older children involves a process any different in kind from that in younger, preoperational children.

Attempts to characterize the nature of the developments involved in children's burgeoning language production abilities are rather more difficult,
if only because we are still so far from an understanding of the process of
language production in either children or adults. But there appears to be no
reason whatsoever for believing that there is any basic difference in the ways
in which preoperational and concrete operational children go about the task
of producing utterances. Nor has anyone suggested the existence of a basic
difference in the representation of semantic information in preoperational
and concrete operational children. Thus, there seems to be no evidence of
changes in the nature of linguistic processing during middle childhood that
might parallel the changes so commonly encountered in cognitive tasks.

At this point, one might conclude that linguistic and cognitive development diverge during middle childhood and that the close parallel evident earlier in development does not persist. To do so would require also concluding

that all of the cognitive skills necessary for dealing with language are ones already available to preoperational children and that later linguistic development involves only the continued application of those skills to newly encountered linguistic problems.

An alternative becomes apparent, however, if we approach the cognitive developmental changes of middle childhood from a slightly different standpoint. Most often, those changes are considered in the context of problem situations in which both preoperational and concrete operational children perform systematically, albeit differently. Conservation problems are examples par excellence of this sort. Doing so leads to focusing on the ways in which preoperational and concrete operational children differ in dealing with the same problems and makes it all too easy to ignore the fact that the developmental changes produce differences of another sort as well — that the concrete operational child can deal systematically with a wide variety of cognitive problems for which the preoperational child has *no* systematic approach at all, either correct or incorrect.

To take one small example, it is becoming increasingly apparent that even quite young children are not completely devoid of skills for dealing with number and may, for example, be able to recognize instances of addition and subtraction (see, e.g., GELMAN and GALLISTEL 1978). Bu the numerical skills of such children do not extend to being able to deal in any systematic way with a problem such as $14 + 23 = ?$, let alone being able to multiply or divide. And while at least some of the difference between an older child who can multiply and a younger one who cannot is certainly an increase in knowledge, some of it is also an increase in the variety of problems with which the older child can cope.

Thus, one aspect of the developmental changes occurring during middle childhood involves an increase in the variety of things children can do. And this suggests that perhaps the linguistic development we are seeking in middle childhood is a development of the same sort — the emergence of an ability to deal with additional linguistic problems rather than a change in the manner of dealing with old ones.

In fact, the kind of linguistic development most characteristic of middle childhood appears to be a development of just this sort. In addition to adding to their already substantial comprehension and production abilities, children during the transition from preoperational to concrete operational cognitive functioning are also developing a set of *meta*linguistic abilities, abilities that involve reflecting upon the properties of language. But the claim here is stronger in two ways than just that such metalinguistic abilities develop during the same period as the cognitive developmental transition from preoperations to concrete operations. First, it is proposed that the metalinguistic abilities that develop during middle childhood, while superficially disparate, are all manifestations of a single underlying development. Second, it is proposed that this underlying development is the same as that which underlies the development of concrete operational thought. If we are correct, metalinguistic development is best seen as the linguistic manifestation of a general and pervasive cognitive developmental change.

The proposal that middle childhood is the occasion for a flowering of children's metalinguistic abilities is not an entirely novel one. Numerous authors (e.g., CAZDEN 1972, 1975; GLEITMAN 1974; PAPANDROPOULOU and SINCLAIR 1974) have made similar proposals. And the past few years have witnessed an increasing number of studies exploring one or another aspect of children's emerging metalinguistic competence. But such studies have generally been restricted to considering the development of one kind of metalinguistic performance. Consequently, they do not allow evaluating the claim that the emergence of diverse metalinguistic performances represents a single underlying development rather than several independent developments, all of which happen to occur within the same age period. By the same token, such studies cannot provide evidence bearing on the claim that metalinguistic development is a reflection of the same developments that underlie the emergence of concrete operational thought.

The research to be reported here attempts to evaluate these claims by evaluating and interrelating children's performances on three tasks involving metalinguistic abilities and, in addition, a set of tasks assessing concrete operational thinking. Before turning to this research, however, the following chapter will consider a few kinds of metalinguistic performances in terms of the psychological processes and abilities they seem to require. There, the available evidence on the emergence of metalinguistic abilities will be reviewed. That chapter will close with a consideration of the empirical and conceptual relationships that appear to hold between metalinguistic development and the development of concrete operational thought.

Chapter 2   The Nature and Development of Metalinguistic Abilities

As noted at the outset, adults are capable of making a variety of kinds of judgments about utterances. For one, they are capable of noticing that utterances which they or others have produced are, in one way or another, defective. Few would judge Eliot's *The Wasteland* or the blatherings of Lewis Carroll's Jaberwock to be normal, acceptable English.

Certainly, the comprehensibility of an utterance is one consideration entering into a judgment of whether or not it is acceptable. It is, in all likelihood, the difficulty of understanding such doubly self-embedded sentences as (2.1)

The lion the tiger the gorilla chased killed was ferocious.   (2.1)

that leads most hearers to regard them as both incomprehensible and unacceptable. But, as NOAM CHOMSKY (1965) has pointed out, acceptability judgments also reflect evaluations of whether sentences are grammatically well formed and semantically coherent. Numerous sentences that convey their meanings perfectly well are regarded as unacceptable. And though perhaps less frequent, it is certainly not unknown for a listener to have no idea whatsoever of what a speaker was saying without having any inclination to accuse him of speaking nonsense. In this sense, judgments of acceptability are at least quasi-independent of comprehension.

The ability to make such judgments is, of course, neither logically nor psychologically the same as the abilities directly involved in understanding the utterances judged. Listeners more often than not understand the utterances they hear without ever pausing to notice whether or not they were acceptable. Making the judgment that an utterance is or is not acceptable *may* follow upon efforts to understand it, but the judgment does not *necessarily* follow. In this sense, making an acceptability judgment involves processing in addition to comprehension processing, additional processing that is optional, not mandatory. Thus, we cannot infer from the fact that a person gives evidence of understanding utterances that s/he is also able to make acceptability judgments of those utterances. In point of fact, it appears that most adults can, even though they generally do not. But this is a matter of empirical fact, not of logical necessity. And we cannot assume a priori that the facts will be the same for children.

Adult intuitions about ambiguity have somewhat the same character of involving additional, optional processing above and beyond that involved in understanding ambiguous utterances. The available evidence suggests that the presence of an ambiguity in an utterance does exert an influence upon on-line comprehension processing (e.g., FOSS 1970; FOSS and JENKINS 1973; SWINNEY and HAKES 1976). But this influence is not one that leaves a conscious trace. Rarely are we aware that a sentence we have understood was, in fact, ambiguous. Noticing an ambiguity seems to involve additional, post-comprehension processing of a sort that might occur if someone were to ask whether the sentence could have more than one meaning or if a hearer were to discover, after the fact, that s/he has been led down the proverbial garden path.

Similar comments could be made about intuitions about synonymy. Since listeners rarely hear two synonymous sentences in close succession, the occasion for noticing synonymy rarely arises spontaneously. But even when the occasion does arise, hearing and understanding two synonymous sentences neither entails nor necessarily results in the hearer noticing their synonymy.

One characteristic that appears to be common to these and other linguistic intuitions is that the processes underlying the intuitions, while dependent upon comprehension processing, are different from comprehension processes and also from production processes. The processes involved in comprehension seem, in general, to be of the sort which have come recently to be characterized as "automatic" (LABERGE and SAMUELS 1974; SHIFFRIN and SCHNEIDER 1977; SCHNEIDER and SHIFFRIN 1977). Such processes are executed with extreme rapidity and seem also to be relatively invariant in their execution from one occasion to the next. In addition, such processes appear to be inaccessible to awareness.

Such automated information processing operations are generally contrasted with "controlled" operations. The latter involve some sort of "control" or "executive" process, implying an element of choice in whether or not the operations are performed. Such operations are executed relatively slowly and deliberately.

Language comprehension processes (and most phases of production as well) seem clearly to be of the automated sort. Given the rate of speech input and the amount of processing that must intervene between input and comprehension, the processing must proceed with extreme rapidity. Further, during comprehension processing, there is no indication of the listener's having any control over *how* s/he does it. (If there is any choice, it may be in *whether* comprehension processing will occur at all, that is, in whether to listen to the speaker at all.) And listeners are characteristically unaware of anything intervening between their being aware of a speaker's voice and being aware that the message has been understood; even less are listeners able to report on the nature of the intervening processes.

This inaccessibility of comprehension processes to awareness may, in fact, be a characteristic which differentiates them from the kinds of automated processes generally discussed. These are ones that have begun as controlled processes and have become automated after considerable practice. Characteristically, control can be *re*-exerted over such processes, slowing them down but rendering them accessible to awareness. Comprehension processes, on the other hand, give no evidence of ever having been under control or of being capable of being brought under control. In this sense, they may be *inherently* automatic processes.

The processes underlying linguistic intuitions seem quite different from those involved in comprehension. By and large, they appear to be optional in their execution, implying that there is choice involved in whether or not to implement any particular set of such processes. Further, one may deliberate at considerable length and quite consciously over, say, whether a particular sentence is or is not ambiguous. In a sense, then such processes appear to be controlled processes that can be added into the stream of processing after the completion of the automatic comprehension processes.

There have as yet been few attempts to characterize the nature of the processes underlying linguistic intuitions. We can, however, suggest some of the general properties such processes must have. Consider, for example, what must be involved in deciding whether or not two sentences are synonymous. One prerequisite for making such a judgment is certainly having heard and understood two sentences, which we may assume involves forming mental representations of their meanings. In addition, the judgment must involve a comparison of those representations and a decision as to whether they are sufficiently similar that the sentences should be regarded as having the same (or nearly the same) meaning. Thus, to complete a synonymy judgment requires that the listener must compute and retain representations of the sentences' meanings and, further, utilize those representations in a comparison and decision process. It is this latter process that appears to be a controlled process.

However, the process of arriving at a synonymy judgment must be more complex than just a comparison of the semantic representations of two sentences.

If, for example we were to hear a speaker say, "Herb kissed Eve," followed immediately by, "Herb kissed Eve," we would probably not conclude that s/he had uttered two synonymous sentences. Rather, we would be more likely to conclude that s/he had uttered the same sentence twice. Thus, in addition to being able to distinguish pairs of different sentences whose meanings are the same from pairs whose meanings are not, we are also able to distinguish them from pairs consisting of two identical sentences. That is, synonymous pairs are only those whose meanings are the same but whose superficial forms are different. This implies that in addition to comparing the sentences' semantic representations, a synonymy judgment must also involve comparing representations of their superficial forms. If both the superficial and semantic representations of the two sentences match, the two are properly judged to be two tokens of the same sentence. If only the semantic representations match, they are properly judged to be synonymous. And if neither pair of representations matches, they should be judged to be nonsynonymous sentences. (Note that ambiguity judgments can be characterized in a parallel manner: a sentence judged to be ambiguous is one for which there is a match at the superficial level but a mismatch at the semantic level, i.e., a sentence with a single superficial form but two meanings.)

Similar suggestions could probably be developed concerning the processes underlying other linguistic intuitions. But to do so at this point would lead away from the question of central concern: how do such intuitions develop in children?

2.1 The Development of Metalinguistic Abilities

It has been argued thus far that the psychological processes underlying linguistic intuitions, processes involving metalinguistic abilities, are both logically and psychologically distinct from the processes involved in language comprehension and production. Nonetheless, it might still be that such metalinguistic abilities arise as automatic consequences of children's developing comprehension and/or production abilities. It is conceivable, for example, that when children first discover how to understand correctly the meanings of passive sentences, they also immediately notice that for any particular passive there is an active with essentially the same meaning. Do linguistic intuitions develop in this way, or do they have their own separate developmental history?

The kind of intuition that has been the most widely studied, both in adults and developmentally, is acceptability. That such intuitions are not highly developed in young children is a fact familar to anyone who has tried eliciting such judgments or who is familiar with BROWN and BELLUGI's (1964) often-quoted response from a 2½-year old of "Pop goes the weasel!" to a question about the acceptability of "two shoe."

But even quite young children are not completely unable to deal with questions about acceptability. In a seminal paper on metalinguistic development, GLEITMAN et al. (1972) reported an informal experiment in which they attempted to elicit judgments of whether sentences sounded "good" or "silly" from three girls, all about 2½ years old. Well-formed and telegraphic imperatives were used, together with their inverses, such as "Bring me the ball,", "Bring ball," "Ball me the bring," and "Ball bring." All three children judged the well-formed imperatives "good" more often than chance, though less than 100%. The inverted imperatives were less likely to be judged "good" than the well-formed ones; but even the inverted imperatives were more likely to be judged "good" than to be judged "silly." Only one of the children judged the telegraphic imperatives "good" less often than the well-formed ones.

DE VILLIERS and DE VILLIERS (1972) also studied young children's acceptability judgments, using a task in which children judged and corrected utterances produced by a puppet. The sentences used included well-formed and anomalous imperatives, as well as correct-order and reverse-order ones, such as "Throw the stone," "Throw the sky," "Brush your teeth," and "Teeth your brush." Eight children were tested, ranging in age from 28 to 45 months. Nearly all the children judged the anomalous imperatives to be "wrong" more often than their well-formed counterparts. But only the more linguistically mature children judged the reverse-order imperatives to be "wrong" more often than their correct-order counterparts.

The results of these studies suggest that even children under 3 years of age are not wholly incapable of distinguishing well-formed sentences from deviant ones. But the children's criteria appear to be far laxer than those of adults: they accept many sentences that adults would not. The pattern of the results obtained by the DE VILLIERS suggests a reason for this: young children judge on a basis different from adults.

As noted earlier, several studies of young children's comprehension performance have found that young children are relatively insensitive to the order in which words occur in a sentence. Their results suggest that 2½-year-olds consider mainly the meanings of a sentence's content words, fitting them together in any way that makes sense. Only later does the strategy of using word order as a clue to a sentence's meaning become a part of children's repertoires of comprehension strategies.

Considering the sentences used by GLEITMAN et al. and the DE VILLIERS in terms of the comprehension strategies available to young children, it appears that there is a direct relationship between the sentences they find acceptable and those they think they understand. Children who do not yet use word-order information in comprehension should "understand" both well-formed and reverse-order imperatives. But since, for anomalous imperatives, there is no arrangement of the words that makes sense, these should not be understood. Later, when the word order strategy develops, children should also find reverse-order imperatives unintelligible. Hence, the fact that the DE VILLIERS' younger, less mature subjects rejected only the anomalous imperatives, while their more mature subjects and, to some extent, the subjects in the GLEITMAN et al. study, rejected both the anomalous and reverse-order imperatives follows directly from facts about young children's developing comprehension strategies. The data suggest that young children accept sentences they think they understand; they do not accept sentences they find incomprehensible. As their comprehension abilities develop, the pattern of sentences accepted and rejected changes accordingly. DE VILLIERS and DE VILLIERS (1974) provided some evidence for this interpretation of the children's acceptability judgments in a later study, finding a correlation of +0.77 between children's word-order corrections and their comprehension of reversible passives.

The results of these studies suggest that even quite young children have some nascent metalinguistic ability. They appear to be aware, at least some of the time, of whether they have understood what a speaker said. By the same token, however, this ability must be viewed as only a very rudimentary form of the acceptability-judging ability adults possess. As we noted earlier, comprehensibility is only one of the considerations entering into adult judgments. And, for most sentences, it plays a role secondary to grammatical and semantic considerations. That is, adult judgments often have a character something like, "I know what he's trying to say, but he didn't say it *right*." Thus, developmentally there appears to be a change in the criteria on which acceptability judgments are based.

There are numerous studies that have examined acceptability judgments in somewhat older children (e.g., BOHANNON 1975, 1976; GLEITMAN et al., 1973; HOWE and HILLMAN 1973; JAMES and MILLER 1973; SCHOLL and RYAN 1975). Such studies have generally collected data from children of 5 years or more, leaving a gap in the age distribution studied. [One exception is a recent study by CARR (1979), who examined judgments longitudinally in children between 2;0 and 5;0. This study will be considered shortly.] In general, the results of the studies of older children suggest that children come gradually to make judgments more and more like those of adults, especially in terms of rejecting more and more sentences that adults find unacceptable. But these studies provide few insights into the bases on which children are making their judgments (e.g., the extent to which they are using the comprehensibility criterion of the younger children).

It should be noted in passing that there is considerable variation among these studies in the ages at which they suggest children become able to reject deviant sentences. HOWE and HILLMAN, for example, found that even their 4-year-olds showed some ability to discriminate between sentences that violated animate selectional restrictions and ones that did not. BOHANNON (1975), on the other hand, concluded that "... the majority of first-grade children *cannot* discriminate syntax" (emphasis added) in an experiment comparing sentences with normal word order with ones in which the words had been randomly rearranged.

It appears that an important difference between these two studies, a difference that differentiates among other studies as well, is a methodological one. HOWE and HILLMAN began by presenting their subjects with grossly anomalous sentences and asking them to describe what was wrong with them. Having elicited the children's own terms (which included "bad," "silly," "wrong," "stupid," "make believe," and "doesn't make sense"), they then asked the children to evaluate sentences using these same terms. BOHANNON, in contrast, presented his subjects with pictures of two people, asking them to identify normal sentences as having been spoken by one of them and scrambled sentences by the other. Intuitively, the latter seems a far more difficult task, and the difference in results may well be attributable to this difference.

One hint as to the basis on which the children in these studies may have been making their judgments comes from the study by GLEITMAN et al. They obtained acceptability judgments ("good" vs "silly") for a variety of grammatical and ungrammatical sentences from children between 5 and 8 years. In addition, the children were asked to explain their judgments. One 5-year-old judged the sentence "I am eating dinner" to be unacceptable, explaining that he didn't like to eat dinner. As GLEITMAN et al. observed, this seems to be a judgment of what the sentence asserts rather than of the sentence itself, suggesting that the child had difficulty in treating the sentence as a linguistic object to be evaluated in its own right.

A similar suggestion comes from the recent longitudinal study by CARR (1979) of the judgments of children between 2;0 and 5;0. CARR noted that early in the study the children rejected many sentences that adults find acceptable and suggested that they were judging on the basis of their experience with the world, that is, a sentence (grammatical or not) that described something outside the child's likely experience would be judged unacceptable. Unfortunately, CARR did not ask her subjects to explain the bases of their judgments, so we cannot be certain if her inference is correct about the basis for the judgments.

If CARR is correct, however, then her younger subjects appear to have been judging on a basis similar to that suggested by GLEITMAN et al.'s 5-year-old. The suggestion here is that younger children judge, among sentences they understand, on the basis of *what* the sentence asserts or describes rather than judging whether the sentence is an acceptable means for asserting that. Since most investigators have not asked their subjects to explain their judgments, their results cannot be brought to bear on the question of the basis on which the judgments were made.

That children (at least younger ones) may encounter difficulty in dealing with sentences as linguistic objects per se is, however, suggested by the results of a study of a different sort. PAPANDROPOULOU and SINCLAIR (1974; see also BERTHOUD-PAPANDROPOULOU 1978) examined children's concepts of spoken words. When asked to name a "long" word, a typical answer from 4- and 5-year-olds was "train," a short word that names a long object. When asked for a short word, such children gave responses like "primula," a word that is three syllables long but names a very small flower. PAPANDROPOULOU and SINCLAIR asserted, though without presenting their data, that such "content-oriented" responses did not occur for older children. MARKMAN (1976) has also found evidence of a difficulty among kindergarteners and first graders in distinguishing between words and their referents.

Thus, it appears that younger children may be focusing on the "things" named or described linguistically rather than on the linguistic means used for naming or describing them. Further, it appears that this tendency may disappear (or at least diminish) during middle childhood. If so, we may be beginning to gain a glimpse of the nature of the metalinguistic developmental change occurring during this period. The change appears to involve an increasing ability to focus attention upon and evaluate the properties of the language per se.

Children's judgments of synonymy also yield evidence of a change occurring during middle childhood. BEILIN and his associates (BEILIN and SPONTAK 1969;

SACK and BEILIN 1971; see also BEILIN 1975) have performed two experiments bearing on children's emerging intuitions about synonymy. BEILIN and SPONTAK focused on reversible active and passive sentences, assessing comprehension with a picture selection task and assessing synonymy judgments with, among other measures, a direct question task in which two sentences were read to a child, who was then asked whether they meant the same thing or different things. The results indicated that first grade children performed at or below chance on synonymous active-passive pairs, as did younger children. That is, they were at least as likely to say that the sentences meant different things as to say that they meant the same thing. Only the second graders performed significantly better than chance. Essentially the same developmental pattern was found for pairs composed of an active sentence and a subject-object reversal of that sentence, a case for which the correct judgment was that they did not mean the same thing. Comparison of the results for the synonymy task with those for the comprehension task indicates that synonymy performance improved rather later than comprehension performance.

SACK and BEILIN provided further evidence that the ability to judge synonymy emerges later than the ability to understand the sentences being judged. Using active and passive sentences and also subject-cleft and object-cleft sentences, they collected data on comprehension, recognition, recall, and synonymy tasks. The comprehension data showed that even the youngest subjects (nursery school children) performed better than chance on the actives, passives, and subject clefts, though even the oldest children (second graders) did not perform consistently well with the object clefts. On the recognition task, even the youngest children showed better recognition of sentences they had heard before than of new sentences with the same grammatical structures. Children of all ages studied were more likely than chance to recognize *falsely* new sentences that were synonymous with, but different in syntactic form from, sentences they had heard before, demonstrating that even nursery school children were extracting the same meanings from active and passive sentences and, to some extent, from subject- and object-cleft sentences. These recognition data are important, for without demonstrating that synonymous sentences are confused in memory and, hence, have essentially the same memory representation, it could be argued that the younger children did not judge such sentence pairs to be synonymous simply because they computed different semantic representations for them.

For the synonymy task, the active-passive pairs yielded results very similar to those of the BEILIN and SPONTAK study. Again, through first grade, performance was at or below chance, rising above chance only for the second graders. For the subject- and object-cleft pairs, performance was at or below chance for all age groups, most likely reflecting the poor comprehension of the object clefts.

The results of both these studies suggest that there is a substantial development during middle childhood of children's ability to judge synonymy and that this development occurs later than the development of the ability to understand the sentences judged. Further, they also suggest that younger children (i.e., first graders and younger) may perform systematically worse than chance on synonymous sentence pairs. If this is the case, it suggests that the developmental change underlying the emergence of adultlike synonymy judgments, like that underlying the development of adultlike acceptability judgments, involves a change in the basis on which children make their judgments.

Research on children's ability to judge that sentences are ambiguous also suggests that this ability increases considerably during middle childhood and even beyond (KESSEL 1970; SHULTZ and PILON 1973). Although neither of these studies involved children younger than 6 years, the performance of the 6-year-olds was sufficiently poor for all the kinds of ambiguities tested that testing even younger children would probably not have been productive.

It should be noted, however, that intuitions about ambiguity are extremely difficult to study. Judging a sentence to be ambiguous requires judging that, in addition to having one structure and meaning that are acceptable, the sentence has at least one additional acceptable structure and meaning. Clearly, this is a more complex judgment than one of acceptability. In addition, it is extremely difficult to design a task adequate for eliciting ambiguity judgments. The task used both by KESSEL and by SHULTZ and PILON leaves much to be desired in this respect (see EVANS 1976). For both of these reasons, it seems well advised to be cautious in making claims about when and how intuitions about ambiguity emerge. Nonetheless, the evidence suggests that such intuitions show considerable development during and after middle childhood.

Consonant with this are data from a number of studies (e.g., BRODZINSKY 1977; FOWLES and GLANZ 1977; HIRSH-PASEK et al. 1978; SHULTZ and HORIBE 1974) suggesting that there is a considerable development during this same period in children's ability to understand and appreciate verbal jokes and riddles. For example, the humor of the riddle, "Why was the little strawberry crying?" "Because his mom and pop were in a jam," rests in part on the incongruity of a strawberry crying but also on the resolution of the incongruity that arises in noticing the ambiguity of "jam" (see MCGHEE 1977; SHULTZ 1976). So it seems reasonable to suppose that the emergence of an understanding of jokes and riddles reflects the child's emerging sensitivity to the ambiguities upon which they depend.

It was noted earlier that young children tend to respond to questions about spoken words in terms of properties of the words' referents rather than properties of the words themselves, a tendency that diminishes markedly during middle childhood. Consistent with this are the results of a number of other studies that have examined other aspects of children's knowledge of spoken words, both in isolation and in sentences. For example, ROZIN et al. (1974) found that kindergarten children and many first and second graders had difficulty matching long and short spoken words with their written representations, suggesting that they are unable to deal with spoken words in terms of their length (see also LUNDBERG and TORNEUS 1978). Similarly, children of these ages often encounter difficulty in segmenting spoken phrases and sentences into their component words and sounds (e.g., DOWNING and OLIVER 1973-74; FOX and ROUTH 1975, 1976; HOLDEN and MACGINITIE 1972).

LIBERMAN et al. (1974) have also presented data suggesting that children encounter a special difficulty in dealing explicitly with the sound units in spoken words. They developed a task for assessing children's ability to count the numbers of segments in spoken words and syllables. The experimenter spoke a word and asked the child to tap out the number of segments it contained, the experimenter providing examples of what was desired. For syllabic segments, for example, the experimenter said a one-syllable word (e.g., "but"), tapping once, and then asking the child to repeat the word and tap it in the same way. A two-syllable word was then presented (e.g., "butter"), with two taps, followed by a three-syllable word (e.g., "butterfly"), with three taps. If the child made a mistake, the experimenter again demonstrated the correct number of taps.

After several trials on which the experimenter demonstrated the correct number before asking the child to tap, there were 42 trials on which the child was asked to tap one-, two-, and three-syllable words without prior demonstration. The experimenter continued to demonstrate the correct number if the child made an error. Thus, the task was a learning task, the question being whether the child could learn that the correct number of taps was determined by the number of syllables in the word. Learning, therefore, was dependent upon the child's being able to determine the number of syllables each word contained.

LIBERMAN et al. also developed a parallel task involving phonemic segmentation. Here, for example, /u/ was one tap, "boo" was two, and "boot" was three. Thus, learning in this latter task was dependent upon the child's being able to determine the number of segmental phonemes in syllables. All the syllables used contained one, two, or three phonemes.

Groups of nursery school, kindergarten, and first grade children were tested on the syllabic and phonemic segmentation tasks, different children receiving the two tasks. The phonemic task was considerably more difficult than the syllabic task. At the nursery school level, 46% of the children reached criterion (six consecutive correct responses) on the syllabic task; none did so on the phonemic task. At the kindergarten level, the comparable percentages were 48 and 17; and at the first grade level, they were 90 and 70. Being aware of the phonemic structure of spoken words or syllables appears to be beyond the capabilities of 4-year-olds and is generally, though not universally, within the capabilities of children by the time they reach the end of the first grade. Being aware of the syllabic structure of spoken words is apparently a capability that develops rather earlier.

It is worth noting that a number of studies have implicated a lack of awareness of the spoken language's phonemic level of analysis in the difficulties encountered by many first graders in learning to read (see, e.g., GLEITMAN and ROZIN 1973; LIBERMAN et al. 1977; SAVIN 1972; TREIMAN and BARON, in press; ZIFCAK 1978). This again suggests that this sort of "phonological awareness" does not emerge until middle childhood and, for some children, may be delayed even further.

On first consideration, these results concerning phonological awareness seem paradoxical. Children must surely be able to construct representations of the phonological content of heard utterances much earlier than these data suggest, for this is prerequisite to understanding utterances. Research by SHVACHKIN (1973), GARNICA (1973), and others, as well as an abundance of everyday observations, suggests that children are able to use phonological differences between spoken words to signal meaning differences at an age far younger than the age at which phonological awareness appears to emerge.

The resolution to the paradox lies in the fact that using a phonological difference to signal a meaning difference is not the same as realizing that the relevant difference is a phonological one. The former requires discriminating auditory patterns that, in fact, differ phonologically; the latter involves discovering that *that* is the relevant way in which such patterns differ. Thus, a child who is quite well able to tell that "cat" and "bat" are different words need not be aware that each is composed of three segments and that it is only in the first segment that the two differ.

Even so, it is not immediately obvious why children should not be able to deal explicitly with a spoken utterance's phonological units until later than they are able to deal with its syllabic units. An adequate account of the reasons for this difference is not yet available (but see HIRSH-PASEK et al. 1978; LIBERMAN et al. 1977). Nonetheless, it seems likely that at least a part of such an account will concern differences in the nature of these units themselves.

Speech researchers and theorists have often observed that segmental phonemes (or phonological feature matrices) do not correspond in any simple way to segments of the acoustic signals constituting speech (see, e.g., LIBERMAN et al. 1967). That is, it is not possible to segment a speech signal such that each segment corresponds to one and only one phoneme. Rather, any portion of the signal is likely to convey information about more than one phonemic segment, a property often referred to as "parallel transmission." In this sense, phonological segments do not exist in the acoustic signal itself; they must be constructed from that signal.

Syllabic segments appear to have a somewhat different status. The minimal acoustic segment that consistently conveys phonological information is the syllable. Further, it appears that there are acoustic properties that signal and differentiate syllabic segments. So, in a sense, syllables exist in the acoustic signal itself and are more transparent to the speech perceiver than are phonemes. (Note that this does not imply that listeners can necessarily locate syllable boundaries with accuracy. They often cannot. Rather, it implies that the *number* of syllables is information made available by the processes involved in speech perception. But it is the number of units, rather than their boundaries, that is at issue in tasks involving syllabic or phonemic awareness.)

The suggestion, then, is that syllabic units are inherent products of speech perception processing while phonemic units are not. To the extent that the latter units must be constructed out of the products of speech perception processing, it seems reasonable that they should be less accessible and, hence, discovered later in life than syllabic units. Consistent with this developmental difference is also the fact that even for adults, syllabic units are more readily accessible than phonemic units. For example, if adults are asked to listen to a sequence of syllables and respond as quickly as possible to the occurrence of either a specified syllable or a specified syllable-initial phoneme, response times are shorter for whole syllables than for their initial phonemes (e.g., FOSS and SWINNEY 1973; SAVIN and BEVER 1970).

Additional indirect evidence for the emergence of phonological awareness during middle childhood may be found in studies of abilities which presuppose such awareness. Sensitivity to rhyme should be such an ability, for a rhyming pair of words is (roughly) one in which the initial phonemes differ while the remaining phonemes do not. KNAFLE (1974) has found a substantial increase in children's ability to discriminate between rhyming word pairs and nonrhyming pairs between kindergarten and third grade. JUSCZYK (1977) has also found differences in the ability to deal with rhyming between first and third graders.

The same sort of development most likely underlies the emergence in middle childhood of an appreciation of puns (see, e.g., MCGHEE 1974), a form of humor partially dependent upon the phonological properties of words. For example, whatever humor value "The bun is the lowest form of pastry" has derives both from its parallel with "The pun is the lowest form of humor" and from the phonological similarity of "bun" and "pun."

The results of these studies of rhyming and phonological awareness seem inconsistent with the fact that WEIR (1962) and others (see CLARK 1978) have observed that considerably younger children (e.g., 2-year-olds) often engage in "sound substitution drills" in which they produce sequences of rhyming sound patterns. There is, however, no particular reason to believe that this early "rhyming" involves an analysis of sound sequences into phonological units. The 2-year-old could equally well be manipulating larger (e.g., syllabic) units. Further, this early spontaneous "rhyming" may well not involve children's being aware of the phonological properties of the sound sequences they are producing. That is, 2-year-olds may produce sequences of sounds that do in fact rhyme, but it is unclear that they know that *that* is what they are doing.

Results reported by ZHUROVA (1973) might seem to call into question the claim that it is not until middle childhood that children become able to deal explicitly with the phonological units in spoken words. ZHUROVA attempted to teach children as young as 3 years to separate the sounds in words. Although she reported some success with 3- and 4-year-olds (and considerably more success with older children), it appears that the accomplishments of the 3- and 4-year-olds were quite limited, extending only to separating a word's initial sound from the remainder, and this only under highly constrained conditions. [Interestingly, ZHUROVA met with even less success trying to teach children to separate a word's final segment from its remainder. Parallel with this difference between initial and final sounds is a result obtained by JUSCZYK (1977): first, second, and third graders show less ability to deal with alliteration than with rhyme. It may be that when phonological awareness begins to emerge it emerges first and best for the beginnings of words.]

Still another metalinguistic domain in which considerable developmental changes appear to occur during middle childhood is that involving dealing with language nonliterally, that is, understanding such devices as metaphor and simile (see, e.g., BILLOW 1975; COMETA and ESON 1978; GARDNER et al. 1978). This development bears an interesting parallel to that for rhyming. WINNER (1979; see also CHUKOVSKY 1963) has argued persuasively that many utterances produced by quite young children have the characteristics of metaphors, for example, "I putting on your clothes, crayon," was said by a 2½-year-old while sliding the paper cover on a crayon after it had slipped off. Yet the abilities involved in thinking about metaphor, that is, explaining metaphors and discriminating metaphors from nonmetaphors, appear to emerge only considerably later. As in the case of rhyming, this development raises an interesting question about the ways in which children's early metalinguistic performance differ from later ones, a question to be considered later.

In any event, there are a number of lines of evidence that suggest the occurrence of major developmental changes during middle childhood in children's abilities to deal with a variety of tasks that require reflecting upon the properties of language. Unfortunately, most studies have considered developmental changes in only a single kind of metalinguistic performance. So it remains unclear whether all the various metalinguistic abilities that flower during middle childhood are manifestations of a single underlying developmental change or whether they are a set of independent developments which, by coincidence, all happen to occur during the same developmental period.

2.2 Relationships Between Metalinguistic and Cognitive Developments

Just as there is little empirical evidence as yet to link the development of one kind of metalinguistic performance to that of others, there is also little evidence available concerning how the development of metalinguistic abilities might be related to other aspects of cognitive development. Many authors have assumed that such relationships exist, based largely on the similar time courses of metalinguistic and concrete operational developments. But empirical evidence of such relationships is largely lacking, if only because most investigators of metalinguistic development have not simultaneously examined performance on cognitive developmental tasks in the same subjects.

There are, to be sure, a few empirical hints. BEILIN and SPONTAK (1969), for example, included in their study of children's synonymy judgments a task involving operational reversibility, finding that developmental changes in performance on that task paralleled those on the synonymy tasks. SCHOLNICK and ADAMS (1973) have reported a significant correlation between children's performance on a matrix permutation task and their performance on a task involving giving the active equivalents of passive sentences. And BILLOW (1975) and COMETA and ESON (1978) have found relationships between performance on Piagetian concrete operational tasks and on tasks tapping an understanding of metaphors.

The existence of a metalinguistic-cognitive developmental relationship can also be inferred indirectly from data on phonological awareness, reading achievement, and concrete operations. ZIFCAK (1978) has reported a substantial relationship between first graders' performance on the LIBERMAN et al. phoneme segmentation task and reading achievement (see also TREIMAN and BARON, in press). LUNZER et al. (1976) have reported a similar relationship between reading achievement and an "operativity" factor derived from several Piagetian tasks. Given the magnitude of the relationships between reading achievement and each of these, it seems highly unlikely that the contributions of phonological awareness and operativity to reading achievement are independent of each other.

There are, then, a few empirical suggestions of a common denominator underlying aspects of metalinguistic development and aspects of the development of concrete operational functioning. But as yet these are no more than tantalizing hints. And they do not speak to the question of what such a common denominator might be. That is, are there conceptual as well as empirical reasons for believing metalinguistic development to be the linguistic reflection of the emergence of concrete operations?

One fairly obvious parallel is suggested by the characterization given earlier of what is required to successfully execute a synonymy judgment. Such a judgment requires not only forming and retaining representations of the form and meaning of two sentences but, in addition, comparing those representations. This process sounds remarkably similar in its cognitive requirements to the sort of decentering that is involved in the child's "mentally standing back" from and reflecting upon the relationships between properties and states of conservation tasks that are crucial to developing and understanding of conservation.

There is, however, another sort of parallel that is perhaps more suggestive of the nature (if not the causes) of the developmental changes underlying the emergence of both metalinguistic and concrete operational abilities. It was suggested earlier that the common denominator underlying all of the various metalinguistic abilities is that they involve reflecting upon one or another aspect of language per se. This, as CAZDEN (1972, 1975) has pointed out, is not the normal, everyday way in which we deal with language. In producing utterances, the task of main concern is effectively communicating the meaning we intend, not on whether the utterance used to do so is ambiguous, contains a rhyme, or is synonymous with some other possible utterance.

Similarly, upon hearing an utterance, the normal thing to do is to understand it, to "get out its meaning," rather than to think about how the speaker conveyed that meaning. Language, that is, is something normally treated in an *instrumental* manner rather than as an end in itself. As has often been observed, the primary function of language is communication. Understanding an utterance is something we normally do because of the other activities that doing so makes possible, such as acting upon the message conveyed, storing it away for future reference, pondering its implications, searching for the information needed to answer the question posed, and so forth. And all of this requires treating the language itself as "transparent," something to be seen through, rather than as "opaque," something to be focused on in its own right.

There is, of course, a considerable utility in treating language in this transparent manner. Metalinguistic activities are, as noted earlier, slow, deliberate, attention-consuming controlled activities. And, given the rate at which linguistic input typically occurs, pausing to engage in one of these activities is almost certain to disrupt the activities that normally follow upon comprehension as well as to interfere with the comprehension of further input. It seems to be a characteristic of the speech perception and comprehension system that we cannot "hold" the processing of one utterance while we reflect upon a preceding one. Even in reading, where we have the luxury of controlling the rate of input, pausing to reflect upon *how* an author has conveyed a particular piece of the message frequently results in losing the train of thought.

Given these characteristics of metalinguistic activities, what should we expect to find developmentally necessary for a child to be able to engage in them? Certainly, many metalinguistic performances require knowledge of particulars about the language. It is, for example, inconceivable that children should be able to give correct synonymy judgments before they have learned to understand the particular sentences involved. Similarly, making an adult-like acceptability judgment of a particular sentence would seem to presuppose having acquired some knowledge of the rules relevant to that sentence — the rules determining whether or not *that* sentence is grammatical. The implication is, of course, that we should expect to find in the development of metalinguistic abilities the sorts of horizontal décalages between and within tasks that are familiar in other cognitive domains, décalages that arise because of differences in the linguistic knowledge requirements of different tasks and of different items within tasks.

It is, however, common to all metalinguistic activities that they are controlled activities. Engaging in one or another of them involves an element of choice, at least in the sense of having to decide whether or not to interrupt the ongoing stream of normal processing to engage in one of these activities and, if so, which one. There is, that is, a deliberate choice made to place one's self at a distance from the language in order to think *about* it. Thus, we should expect to find the development of metalinguistic abilities marked by increases in children's ability to engage in these sorts of deliberate, controlled mental activities.

It is just these sorts of changes that also seem to characterize the development of "reflected abstraction" (PIAGET 1976, 1978) and to underlie an increasing ability to decenter, to mentally stand back from a situation in order to think about the relationships it involves.

Earlier, in discussing the developmental changes that occur in conservation task performance, it was suggested that one aspect of the change was an increase in cognitive flexibility. That is, preoperational children have no alternative but to approach such tasks with the heuristic inferential strategies they have available. Concrete operational children, however, also have available to them an increasing ability to deal systematically with the relationships involved and, thus, to approach the same situation in more than one way.

Such an increase in cognitive flexibility implies an increase in control of the sort commonly associated with controlled processing, for the concrete operational child is forced, by having multiple approaches to the same problems, to choose which of those approaches to use. Thus, one aspect of the development common to metalinguistic abilities and concrete operational abilities is an increasing ability to act and think deliberately and, concomitantly, to place one's self mentally at a distance from a situation and to reflect upon it. Such a characterization seems to be implicit in many of the recent discussions of "metacognitive" developments during middle childhood (e.g., FLAVELL's 1977 discussion of the development of metamemory). And PIAGET (1976, 1978) suggested many of the same characteristics in his recent discussions of the development of reflected abstraction during middle childhood.

Both metalinguistic and concrete operational development involve an increasing ability to control the course of one's own thought. The change is from a relatively automatic, relatively spontaneous application of the sorts of heuristic strategies available early to a more controlled, more deliberate choice between those processes and others that are available *only* by choice.

There are, then, sufficient parallels between the cognitive abilities required for engaging in metalinguistic activities and those required for concrete operational functioning to suggest that the emergence of a common set of abilities underlies both kinds of development. At this point, this is no more than a suggestion. Making it more than a suggestion would require both empirical evidence of such a developmental relationship and an account of the nature and course of the underlying developments. As yet, neither has been provided. But the intent here has been merely to suggest the existence of both empirical and conceptual reasons for believing that a developmental relationship between metalinguistic and concrete operational abilities might exist. If so, the next question is whether additional empirical evidence concerning the emergence of metalinguistic abilities will be consistent with the view suggested here.

Before turning to the empirical question, however, it is necessary to make clear the nature of the developmental relationships hypothesized. We should not expect to find the development of a metalinguistic ability to be a discontinuous development, either temporally or conceptually. It has already been suggested that horizontal décalages should exist, even within a particular metalinguistic task. If the underlying development responsible for the emergence of metalinguistic abilities is, as suggested, an increase in control over cognitive activities, it seems reasonable to suppose that such control would itself emerge gradually.

Similarly, we cannot expect to find synchrony between the attainment of any particular metalinguistic performance and that of any particular concrete operational performance. The reasons are the same as those suggested earlier for not expecting synchrony during the preoperational period between the acquisition of any particular language comprehension strategy and any particular cognitive developmental change.

In sum, it would be unreasonable to expect to find an age or cognitive developmental level below which children gave no evidence of metalinguistic abilities. It is more reasonable to expect that in both the metalinguistic and cognitive domains there will be gradual increases in ability seen across an increasingly broad range of situations. Some of these changes may be synchronous with others. But this need not be the case. Rather, if the developmental changes in the whole gamut of metalinguistic and concrete operational abilities have a common underlying source, we should expect to find those changes to be correlated. That is, the child whose performance is advanced on one should be advanced on all.

Chapter 3 A Study of Children's Metalinguistic Abilities: Method

One hundred children, 20 each of ages 4, 5, 6, 7, and 8 years, were tested. Each child received a series of five tasks over several short testing sessions. The tasks, in the order in which they were administered, were conservation, comprehension, synonymy, acceptability, and phonemic segmentation. The reason for including the comprehension task lies in the nature of the synonymy task. For this reason, the synonymy task will be described before the comprehension task. The other tasks will be described in the order in which they were administered.

In general, the motivation for selecting the particular metalinguistic tasks used was to sample a variety of apparently important metalinguistic abilities. Synonymy and acceptability were selected because of the prominent role these, together with ambiguity, have played in linguistic discussions of the adult's linguistic competence. (Ambiguity was not included because of the difficulty, mentioned earlier, of devising an appropriate task.) Phonemic segmentation was included because it seemed to require abilities at least superficially quite different from those involved in judgments of synonymy or acceptability. Its inclusion allowed determining whether, despite the superficial differences, performance on this task was related to that on the other metalinguistic and cognitive tasks.

Concrete operational abilities were assessed with a set of conservation tasks. Ideally, the study would have included a greater variety of concrete operational tasks (e.g., seriation, classification, etc.), and a greater variety of metalinguistic tasks as well. The sampling of tasks was limited by two considerations. First, it seemed desirable to collect a sufficient amount and variety of data *within* each of the types of tasks to obtain stable measures of children's performances. Second, there was a limit to the total amount of data that could reasonably be expected to be obtained from an individual child before losing the attention and cooperation necessary for obtaining valid data. It was anticipated that, particularly for the younger subjects, this would be a rather severe constraint. And since, if a child did not provide useable data for all of the tasks, none of that child's data would be useable, this was an important limiting consideration.

3.1 Tasks and Materials

3.1.1 Conservation

The conservation tasks used were the six included in the Goldschmid-Bentler Concept Assessment Kit — Conservation, Form A (GOLDSCHMID and BENTLER 1968). The tasks were designed to evaluate conservation performance in six situations — two-dimensional space, number, substance, continuous quantity, weight, and discontinuous quantity — using standardized materials, instructions, and scoring procedures. Each task involved the experimenter's creating two arrays that were equal in the relevant property and then altering an irrelevant property of one of the arrays. Each task was scored for both the correctness of the child's judgment and the adequacy of the explanation given for that judgment. The scoring criteria were those set forth by GOLDSCHMID and BENTLER.

3.1.2 Synonymy

Previous research on children's synonymy judgments has dealt only with active, passive, subject-cleft, and object-cleft sentences. The intent here was to sample a wider variety of sentence types to ensure that any developmental trends observed would not be peculiar to some particular instance of the synonymy relationship. An obvious constraint on the selection of sentence types was that all of the sentences be ones for which there was a reasonable expectation that they would be understood by children of the ages tested. Asking children whether two sentences mean the same thing when they do not yet understand one or both of the sentences does not yield any information on their ability to judge synonymy. It was for this reason that a comprehension task was included in the battery presented to the children.

A problem that arises in the selection of types of sentence pairs used to exhibit synonymy relations is the lack of a well-specified basis for deciding what counts as synonymy. Views on synonymy appear to be conditioned by views on the nature of meaning, a concept on which there is nothing even approaching a consensus view. In addition, it may be that synonymy, like acceptability, exists in degrees and perhaps is even of several different kinds.

Table 3.1. Types of sentence pairs included in the synonymy task

Sentence pair type	Number of cases	
	Synon.	Nonsynon.
I) Active-passive-cleft	6	6
The nurse was called by the doctor. It was the nurse that the doctor called.		
II) Existentials	4	4
There is an apple on the table. The table has an apple on it.		
III) Temporal relations	6	6
The little boy fed the dog before he watched television. After the little boy fed the dog, he watched television.		
IV) Spatial relations	4	8
The old lady is in front of the boy. The boy is behind the old lady.		
V) Size-amount	6	12
There is more cake than ice cream. There is less ice cream than cake.		

Given the difficulty of arriving at a rigorous specification of synonymy, an easier course was chosen. The types of sentence pairs selected to exemplify synonymy relationships were ones that "the man in the street" would accept as "meaning essentially the same thing" — clear cases of synonymy. The pairs selected to be nonsynonymous were derived from the synonymous pairs, and were equally clear cases of nonsynonymy.

Published studies of children's comprehension performance, as well as pilot comprehension studies performed prior to the present study, allowed identifying five useable sets of synonynous sentence types. These five, together with examples of the sentence pairs used, are presented in Table 3.1.

Active, Passive, and Cleft Sentences

The first set of synonymous sentence pairs included all six possible combinations of active, passive, subject-cleft, and object-cleft sentences. The pairs included both synonymous and nonsynonymous pairs representing each combination, yielding a total of 12 sentence pairs involving these constructions. All the sentences were reversible, in that the subject and object noun phrases (NPs) in each sentence could be interchanged to produce another sentence that was both intelligible and plausible.

Two forms of the synonymy task were constructed. This allowed using a greater number of different sentences, providing some assurance that the results would not be artifacts of the particular sentences used. The sentence pairs on the two forms were related in that each synonymous pair on one form provided the basis for a nonsynonymous pair on the other form, produced by interchanging the subject and object NPs of one sentence of the pair.

The results of available comprehension studies (e.g., BEILIN and SPONTAK 1969; BEVER 1970; SACK and BEILIN 1971) suggested that not all of the youngest subjects (4-year-olds) could be expected to understand all the sentence types in this set, passives and object clefts presenting the greatest likelihood of difficulty. For this reason, passives, subject clefts, and object clefts were included in the comprehension task.

If a child gave evidence on the comprehension task of not understanding one or more of these sentence types, no pairs involving those types were presented to that child in the synonymy task. Rather, sentence pairs composed of the other, comprehended types were substituted. For example, children who failed both the passives and the object clefts on the comprehension task received in the synonymy task only pairs composed of actives paired with subject clefts, some additional pairs of this type being added to replace some of the pairs omitted.

Locative Existential Sentences

The second set of sentence pairs included in the synonymy task comprised pairs of locative existential sentences (see Table 3.1). There are at least the following five such constructions generally regarded as synonymous:

There is a book on the table.
On the table is a book.
On the table there is a book.
A book is on the table.
The table has a book on it.

A pilot comprehension study using children between 3 and 4 years suggested that such children had no difficulty understanding any of the existential forms when used with the locative prepositions "in," "on," and "under." Hence, no examples of these constructions were included in the comprehension task.

Using all possible combinations of the existential constructions for both synonymous and nonsynonymous sentence pairs would result in an inordinately large number of pairs of this type. Since the concern was with the synonymy relationship in general, and since the pilot study gave no hint that some existential constructions would be more difficult than others, a sampling of the possible pairings was used. Four pairs of constructions were selected randomly from among the possible pairs; these served as the basis for both the synonymous and nonsynonymous pairs. Two sentences of each of the constructions involved were composed. Of the eight resulting pairs, four appeared as synonymous pairs on one task form and served as the basis for the nonsynonymous pairs on the other form. For the other four, the assignment to synonymous and nonsynonymous pairing was reversed for the two forms.

Existential sentences present a problem in the creation of nonsynonymous pairs. It is not possible to create a nonsynonymous pair out of a synonymous one by simply interchanging nouns within one of the sentences. Interchanging the nouns from the sentence "There are some tomatoes in the garden" would yield "There is some garden in the tomatoes," a clearly anomalous sentence. For this reason, the nonsynonymous existential pairs had to be created either by changing the object (e.g., "carrots" substituted for "tomatoes") or by substituting a different location (e.g., "basket" for "garden").

This is not an entirely satisfactory solution, for it leaves the possibility that a child might decide that a pair of sentences was not synonymous simply by noticing that one contained a word that the other did not. For this reason, the data for the nonsynonymous existential pairs may not be comparable to those for the nonsynonymous pairs involving other structures. Unfortunately, there seemed to be no other solution.

Temporal Relations Sentences

The third set of sentence pairs consisted of temporal relations sentences of the sort studied by AMIDON and CAREY (1972), CLARK (1971), and others. There are four synonymous constructions in this set, resulting from combining the two orders in which a sentence's two propositions occur with the conjunctions "before" and "after" (see Table 3.1). Pairing each form with every other form yields six kinds of synonymous pairs.

Twelve sentence pairs were composed, including two of each possible synonymous pairing. One of these two was used on each task form as a synonymous pair, the other serving as a basis for a nonsynonymous pair. The nonsynonymous pairs were formed by taking one sentence of a synonymous pair and changing either the order of the propositions or the conjunction, but not both.

For example, "The little boy fed the dog before he watched television" could be changed to either "The little boy watched television before he fed the dog" or "The little boy fed the dog after he watched television." Thus, each task form included twelve temporal relations pairs, six synonymous pairs representing the combinations of the four synonymous structures, and six nonsynonymous pairs derived from the synonymous pairs of the other form.

Several studies have indicated that many 4-year-olds do not yet understand some forms of temporal relations sentences. For this reason, sentences of these four forms were included on the comprehension task. As with the passive and cleft sentences, children who did not correctly understand a particular temporal relations structure in that task were not presented pairs involving that structure in the synonymy task. Pairs based on the other, comprehended forms were substituted. However, if a child did not understand two different temporal relations structures, he received only four pairs on the synonymy task (all involving the two comprehended structures) rather than twelve pairs.

Spatial Relations Sentences

The fourth set of sentence pairs included sentences specifying the spatial relationships between pairs of objects (see Table 3.1). Many prepositions specifying spatial relations occur in natural pairs of antonyms, such as "on top of"-"under." Hence, synonymous sentence pairs can be created by substituting one member of such a pair for the other and also interchanging the NPs specifying the two objects. For example, making the appropriate substitution and interchange on the sentence "The toy train is on top of the blanket" yields "The blanket is under the toy train."

Published data (e.g., CLARK 1973; KUCZAJ and MARATSOS 1975), as well as pilot data collected prior to this study, suggested that even the youngest subjects would correctly understand the pairs "on top of"-"under" and "in front of"-"behind." The sentence pairs used in the synonymy task used only these two pairs of locatives. No spatial relations sentences were included in the comprehension task.

Six pairs of sentences were constructed using each of these pairs of locatives. Two such pairs appeared on each task form as synonymous pairs; the remaining four pairs appeared as nonsynonymous pairs. Nonsynonymous pairs were created either by changing the order of mention of the two objects or by changing the locative to its antonym, but not both, for one of the two sentences in a pair. Two nonsynonymous pairs of each kind were included on each task form. (More nonsynonymous than synonymous pairs were used on the suspicion that the two kinds of nonsynonymous pairs might reveal different kinds of failures to cope with the synonymy relationship. Since the data yielded no evidence of a difference between the two, the basis for the original suspicion need not be detailed and the difference will not be mentioned again.)

Size and Amount Sentences

The final set of pairs comprised sentences specifying the relationships between two different kinds of objects in terms of their sizes or amounts (see Table 3.1). The synonymy relationship results from the existence of antonymous comparative adjectives, such as "bigger"-"smaller." A synonymous pair can be created from a sentence like "The doll is bigger than the puppy" by interchanging the two NPs and substituting the antonymous adjective, yielding "The puppy is smaller than the doll."

The adjective pairs used were "bigger"-"smaller," "longer"-"shorter,", and "more"-"less." Results from several studies (e.g., EILERS et al. 1974; WALES and CAMPBELL 1970) suggested that most of our youngest subjects would be able to understand the first two of these pairs. "More"-"less" is more problematic. Several studies (DONALDSON and BALFOUR 1968; PALERMO 1973, 1974) have suggested that 4-year-olds often do not understand "less" correctly, treating it as a synonym rather than an antonym of "more." More recent research (e.g., CAREY 1978; TREHUB and ABRAMOVITCH 1978) suggests that this apparent systematic misunderstanding of "less" is an artifact. But it remains unclear exactly when the children begin to understand either "more" or "less" correctly. Because of the difficulty of avoiding the artifact that arises in attempts to test the comprehension of these terms, it did not seem feasible to include sentences using them in the comprehension task. In hindsight, it might have been better to have not included "more" and "less" sentence pairs in the synonymy task.

Each of the three adjective pairs was used to construct six pairs of synonymous sentences. Two of these appeared on each task form as synonymous pairs, the other four as nonsynonymous pairs. As in the case of the spatial relations pairs, the nonsynonymous pairs were created by taking one sentence of a synonymous pair and either interchanging its NPs or substituting the antonymous adjective, but not both. (The rationale for including both kinds of nonsynonymous pairs was the same as for the spatial relations pairs. Since nothing came of it in this case either, it will not be mentioned again.)

In sum, the synonymy task included 62 sentence pairs. Of these, 26 were synonymous, the remaining 36 being nonsynonymous. The distribution of these pairs across the five instances of the synonymy relationship we have described is shown in Table 3.1. The sentence pairs were arranged in quasirandom orders, the ordering being different for the two task forms.

The Synonymy Task

The synonymy task was developed by CARLOTA SMITH (unpublished research) and similar to the acceptability task used by DE VILLIERS and DE VILLIERS (1972). The child was first introduced to two small stuffed animals, a dog and a turtle. The child was told that the animals liked to play a game in which the dog would first say something and then the turtle would say the same thing but in a different way. The experimenter then demonstrated the way the animals talked, changing voices for the two and presenting two or more examples of synonymous pairs (of kinds different from those used in the task itself).

The experimenter then told the child that the turtle sometimes liked to try to trick the dog. Instead of saying something that meant the same as what the dog had said, the turtle would try to fool him by saying something really different, something that did not mean the same as what the dog had said. Several examples of the turtle being "tricky" were then presented and discussed with the child in an attempt to ensure that s/he understood what counted as being "tricky." When the experimenter was reasonably certain that the child understood the difference between the turtle's playing the game the way he was supposed to and his being tricky, the child was asked to say each time the dog and turtle talked whether the turtle was answering the way he should or being tricky. The distinction between synonymy and nonsynonymy was, thus, a distinction between "okay" and "tricky."

3.1.3 Comprehension

As indicated earlier, the motivation for including a comprehension task was to try to ensure that the children understood sentences of the constructions used in the synonymy task. The task included passives, subject clefts, object clefts, and the four temporal relations constructions, these being the constructions from the synonymy task about whose comprehension there was the greatest question.

Two sets of materials for the comprehension task were constructed, each of which included two sentences of each of the seven constructions. For each sentence, two pictures were prepared. For the passives, subject clefts, and object clefts, one of the two depicted the action described by the sentence (e.g., "The queen was kissed by the spotted frog"); the other depicted the

Fig. 3.1. Comprehension task pictures for the passive and cleft sentences constructed from "The queen kissed the spotted frog" and for the temporal relations sentences constructed from "After the boy ate his dinner, he read a story"

action described by a subject-object reversal of the sentence (e.g., "The spotted frog was kissed by the queen"). The pair of pictures for this sentence is presented in Fig.3.1.

Two pictures were also prepared for each of the temporal relations sentences. Here, however, each depicted one of the two actions described by the sentence. The pair for the sentence "After the boy ate his dinner, he read a story" is presented in Fig.3.1.

The Comprehension Task

The experimenter introduced the task by showing the child the two pictures for the sentence "The car hit the truck." The child was asked to study the pictures to find out what was happening in them. The sentence was then read, and the child was asked to point to the picture which showed what the sentence said. Only a single practice sentence was used as none of the children evidenced any difficulty in understanding what was expected of them.

Following the practice sentence, the six passive and cleft sentences were presented, the sentences on the two forms of the task being in different random orders. For three of the sentences, the correct picture was the top one; for the other three, it was the bottom one.

The child was given additional instructions before the eight temporal relations sentences were presented. S/he was told that what s/he would hear was about *two* things and that one of them happened first and then the other one happened. S/he was told to listen to the sentence and then to point to the picture that showed which thing happened first. Thus, for the sentence given above, the correct picture is the one depicting the boy eating dinner.

3.1.4 Acceptability

As noted earlier, the notion of unacceptability encompasses a broad spectrum of considerations. Sentences that are syntactically deviant are likely to be regarded as unacceptable, as are ones that are semantically anomalous. In addition, sentences that are difficult to understand, even though they may be grammatical and meaningful on linguistic grounds, are also often judged to be unacceptable. It is, in fact, often moot whether a particular sentence is unacceptable for syntactic reasons, semantic reasons, or reasons of some other sort. This lack of certainty stems in part from the fact that different sources of unacceptability are not mutually exclusive.

The intent in constructing materials for the acceptability task was to sample a variety of kinds of deviant sentences while, at the same time, restricting the selection to sentences which, in their nondeviant forms, would be likely to be familiar to even the youngest subjects. This latter constraint was imposed to eliminate sentences that would be judged unacceptable simply because they were so long or complex that the children found them difficult to understand. That is, the intent was to use only sentences whose deviance clearly had a linguistic source.

Two interrelated sets of 36 sentences were developed for use on two forms of the acceptability task. Two forms were used to provide evidence about the extent to which children's judgments were influence by the particular exemplars used. Of the 36 sentences on each form, 15 were nondeviant and 15 were clearly linguistically deviant for adults. The remaining six sentences were both meaningful and syntactically well formed, but were empirically false. The reason for including these will be discussed later. The kinds of deviant sentences, together with examples, are presented in Table 3.2.

In many cases it is difficult to characterize or even to label the nature of a sentence's deviance. For many deviant sentences there are several possible sources, each involving the violation of a different linguistic rule (or several different rules). For example, the sentence "The carpenter fixed"

Table 3.2. Types of sentences included in the acceptability task

Sentence type	Number
1) Word-order changes	6
The kitten chased the string/*The string chased the kitten	
2) Subcategorization rule violations	
A) Transitive verbs	4
The little girl petted the dog/*The little girl petted	
B) Intransitive verbs	4
The teacher coughed/*The teacher coughed the car	
3) Selectional restriction violations	
A) Subject-verb	4
The woman walked to the store/*The playground walked to the store	
B) Verb-object	4
The teacher read a story/*The teacher read a chicken	
C) Adjective-noun	2
The big rock was in the middle of the road/*The sleepy rock was in the middle of the road	
4) Some-any	4
Some children came to play after school/*Any children came to play after school	
5) Inalienable possession	2
The nurse blinked her eyes/*The nurse blinked the doctor's eyes	
6) Meaningful false	6
The big fish was swimming in the sandbox	

is clearly deviant. But is this because a required direct object has been omitted, leaving an objectless transitive verb, or is it because a transitive verb has been inserted inappropriately in a structure requiring an intransitive verb?

The problem of labelling is obviated to some extent if it is known from what particular nondeviant sentence a deviant sentence was derived. (But note that while this may resolve the labelling problem it does not resolve the problem of characterizing the nature of the deviance in either a linguistically or a psychologically illuminating way.) The construction of the deviant sentences for this task began with well-formed sentences. They were then deformed in specific ways. Hence, the deviant sentences will be labelled in terms of the deformations by which they were produced.

Word-Order Changes

The first deviant sentence type involved a word-order change imposed on a simple active declarative, subject-verb-object sentence by interchanging the subject and object NPs. Since not all subject-object interchanges yield deviant sentences (viz., "The boy hit the ball" and "The ball hit the boy"), additional constraints were imposed on the lexical content of the sentences. Primary among these was that the sentences' verbs require animate subjects but allow inanimate direct objects. Interchanging the animate subject of such a verb with its inanimate object yields a sentence whose subject is inanimate but whose verb requires an animate subject.

If this were the only effect produced by such a word-order change, the resulting deviant sentences could be characterized as involving violations of the selectional restrictions between subjects and verbs (see, e.g., N. CHOMSKY 1965). However, subject-object interchanges generally produce an additional kind of deviance. Essentially, the animate subjects which are appropriate for the verbs are, as direct objects, often highly implausible or impossible. For example, interchanging the subject and object NPs of "The lady bought the fur coat" yields "The fur coat bought the lady." "Fur coat" does not meet the requirement of "buy" for an animate subject; and, in addition, ladies are not the kinds of things generally bought (assuming that 4- to 8-year-olds are unlikely to be familiar with the sense in which "ladies" can be "bought" with such things as fur coats).

In this case, the second source of deviance could be characterized as the violation of a second selectional restriction, that between the verb and its direct object. But it is not clear that this provides a uniform characterization of deviant sentences of this sort. In any event, it is clear that word-order-change sentences generally involve more than a single kind of deviance. For this reason, it was anticipated that their unacceptability might be detected more easily and at a younger age than that of other kinds of deviant sentences.

Six nondeviant, active subject-verb-object sentences were constructed according to the constraints already mentioned and using lexical items likely to be familiar to 4-year-olds. Three of these appeared on one task form in their original nondeviant versions; the other three appeared in their word-order-changed, deviant versions. For the other task form, the assignment of sentences to deviant and nondeviant versions was reversed.

Violations of Strict Subcategorization Rules

The second class of deviant sentences involved violations of strict subcategorization rules (see N. CHOMSKY 1965; DOWNEY and HAKES 1968). Such rules are the constraints which a sentence's underlying phrase structure places upon the classes of words that can appear at the terminal nodes of the phrase marker. For example, a phrase marker whose verb phrase node dominates only a single node labelled "Verb" requires a verb from the subcategory of intransitive verbs. Inserting a transitive verb or one requiring a noun-phrase complement into such a structure would result in a violation of a strict subcategorization rule.

One set of sentences within this class involved sentences whose nondeviant form was that of a simple active subject-verb-object sentence containing a transitive verb that did not also have an intransitive reading. The deviant versions of these sentences were created by omitting their direct objects, yielding sentences like "The boy hit."

The other set of sentences within this class was the converse of the first. The nondeviant sentences were simple active subject-predicate sentences whose main verbs were intransitives that did not have transitive readings (e.g., "The teacher coughed"). Their deviant counterparts were created by adding "direct object" NPs, creating mismatches between the structure defined by the verb and the presence of a direct object (e.g., "The teacher coughed the car").

Four nondeviant sentences of each kind were constructed, and a deviant sentence was derived from each. Two sentences of each kind appeared on one task form in their nondeviant versions; the other two appeared in their deviant versions. The assignment of sentences to deviant and nondeviant versions was reversed for the other task form.

Violations of Selectional Restrictions

The third class of deviant sentences comprised several kinds of sentences which could be characterized linguistically as involving violations of selectional restrictions (see N. CHOMSKY 1965). The words they contained were all of the appropriate syntactic categories (and subcategories) for their structures, but the relationships between the words were not correct.

The first set of this sort contained active subject-predicate sentences whose verbs required animate subjects (e.g., "The woman walked to the store"). The deviant versions of these were created by substituting nonanimate nouns for the animate subject nouns (e.g., "The playground walked to the store").

Two nondeviant sentences of this sort were constructed, and from each a deviant sentence was derived.

The second set of selectional restriction violation sentences was similar to the first. However, their verbs required concrete subjects (e.g., "The glass fell off the table"). The deviant versions of these were created by substituting abstract nouns for the concrete subject nouns (e.g., "The idea fell off the table"). Again, two nondeviant sentences of this sort were constructed, and a deviant sentence was derived from each.

Whereas the first two sets of selectional restriction violation sentences involved the relationship between a sentence's verb and its subject NP, the third and fourth sets involved the relationship between the verb and its direct object NP. The third set consisted of two active subject-verb-object sentences whose verbs required inanimate direct objects (e.g., "The teacher read a story"). The deviant version of these were created by substituting animate nouns for the inanimate object nouns (e.g., "The teacher read a chicken"). The fourth set consisted of two active subject-verb-object sentences whose verbs required concrete direct object nouns (e.g., "The queen ate the cake"). The deviant versions of these involved substituting abstract nouns for the concrete object nouns (e.g., "The queen ate the truth"). The nondeviant and deviant versions of the sentences in these sets were assigned to the task forms in the same manner as for the first two sets of selectional restriction violation sentences.

The last set of sentences in this class involved the relationship between the head noun of an NP and a prenominal adjective which modified it. Two sentences were constructed whose subject nouns were inanimate; these nouns were modified by appropriate adjectives (e.g., "The big rock was in the middle of the road"). To create deviant sentences, the adjectives were replaced by ones that could appropriately modify only animate nouns (e.g., "The sleepy rock was in the middle of the road").

Indeterminates, Indefinites, and Negation

The fourth class of deviant sentences comprised sentences involving the relationship between "some" and "any" and negation (see, e.g., KLIMA and BELLUGI 1966). Basically, the relationship of concern involves the fact that when a sentence contains a negative in conjunction with its auxiliary verb, the indefinite "any" is substituted for the indeterminate "some." (The rules governing negation and indefiniteness are, of course, far more complex than this suggests; they appear to be a source of considerable difficulty even for many adults.)

Two affirmative sentences which contained occurrences of "some" were constructed (e.g., "Some children came to play after school"). Their deviant counterparts were formed by substituting "any" for "some" (e.g., "Any children came to play after school"). Two negative sentences containing occurrences of "any" were also constructed (e.g., "The boy didn't have any cookies in his lunch"). These were rendered deviant by substituting "some" for "any" (e.g., "The boy didn't have some cookies in his lunch"). One deviant and one nondeviant sentence of each kind were assigned to each task form.

Inalienable Possession

The fifth, and last, class of deviant sentences concerned inalienable possession. Two sentences were constructed that described actions of kinds one must perform on oneself (e.g., "The girl held her breath"). The deviant counterparts of these were created by substituting a possessive NP for the possessive pronoun (e.g., "The girl held her mother's breath"). The deviant and nondeviant versions of these sentences were assigned to the two task forms in the same manner as the sentences of the other classes.

To summarize, each form of the acceptability task contained a total of 30 deviant and nondeviant sentences. Of these, 15 were deviant and 15 nondeviant by adult standards, each deviant sentence being paired with a nondeviant sentence of the same type. The distribution of sentences of the various types is presented in Table 3.2.

Meaningful False Sentences

As indicated in Table 3.2, the acceptability task also included a set of sentences that were meaningful and syntactically well formed, but which were not true. Such sentences are generally considered to be acceptable, at least on linguistic grounds. The sentences were, however, slightly odd in that what they asserted was extremely unlikely to be true (e.g., "The big fish was swimming in the sandbox").

These sentences were included in the present study on the basis of a hint in the acceptability judgments collected by GLEITMAN et al. (1972) from children between the ages of 5 and 8 years. A few responses given by their younger subjects suggested that those subjects were unable to evaluate the sentences per se, and were instead evaluating the sentences' assertions. That is, they tended to judge sentences to be unacceptable that were, linguistically, perfectly acceptable but which the children appeared to believe were false (see also CARR 1979).

It seemed desirable to determine if the younger subjects would experience similar difficulties in distinguishing between sentences that were unacceptable because they were ungrammatical or anomalous and sentences that were false. It seemed possible that some false negative judgments might occur for the nondeviant sentences on the acceptability task. But such responses would arise only if children thought that sentences that could be true were not. Hence, such false negative judgments might be quite rare. To increase the likelihood that at least some sentences would be judged to be unacceptable solely on grounds of falsity, the meaningful false sentences were included. The same six sentences of this type were included on both forms of the acceptability task.

Thus, the children judged a total of 36 sentences: 15 deviant sentences, 15 nondeviant sentences, and 6 meaningful false sentences. These were arranged in quasi-random orders, with the restriction that no more than two sentences from the same class, either deviant or nondeviant, should appear consecutively. Different orders were used for the two forms.

The Acceptability Task

The task was a modification of the one used by DE VILLIERS and DE VILLIERS (1972). After a child had played the synonymy task "game" with the dog and turtle, s/he was introduced to a purple elephant, the same kind of toy as the other two. The child was told that the elephant had a problem: sometimes when he said something, he would "say it all the wrong way 'round," like saying "juice the drink, please." The child was asked if that didn't sound "pretty silly." After agreeing that it did (which every child did readily), the child was asked to help the elephant learn to talk right. If the elephant said something the right way, the child was to tell him so. But if the elephant said something the wrong way, the child was to tell him that it was wrong. Further, if the child said that the elephant had said it wrong, s/he was asked to tell the elephant why it was wrong and how he should have said it.

Further examples of the elephant saying things correctly and incorrectly were presented, the deviant sentences being quite blatantly so, until the experimenter was confident that the child understood the general nature of the task. The test sentences were then presented. The entire session was tape-recorded for later analysis of the reasons the children gave when they judged the elephant to have spoken incorrectly.

Thus, the task elicited judgments of acceptability and unacceptability, and in addition attempted to elicit reasons from the children for their judgments of unacceptability. When a statement of a reason was unclear, the experimenter encouraged the child to enlarge upon it in a manner much like that of the Piagetian "clinical method."

Note that the task instructions cast the acceptable-unacceptable distinction in terms of whether the elephant "said it right" or "said it all the wrong way 'round,'" attempting to focus the children's attention on the way the elephant expressed himself rather than on the content of what he said. The description "pretty silly" was also used. And in asking about the acceptability of particular elephant sentences, the terms "right" and "good" and the terms "wrong" and "silly" were used interchangeably. "Good" was suggested as an appropriate thing to say to an elephant when he had said something in an acceptable manner. "Right" and "wrong" are the terms used by the DE VILLIERS (1972) in their study of acceptability judgments, and "good" and "silly" are the terms used by GLEITMAN et al. (1972). Both "wrong" and "silly" are also among the terms elicited by HOWE and HILLMAN (1973) when they asked children to describe deviant sentences.

Attention is called here to the terminology used in the acceptability task because some controversy has arisen about such terminology (see e.g., SCHOLL and RYAN 1975). Since the controversy concerns the effects particular wordings of the acceptable-unacceptable distinction might have on the nature of the children's responses, it will be considered when those responses are discussed.

3.1.5 Phonemic Segmentation

The task used was the one developed by LIBERMAN et al. (1974), and was described earlier. The instructions, examples, and test items were all taken verbatim from LIBERMAN et al. However, only the phonemic segmentation task was used, and not the parallel syllabic segmentation task. The available data on syllabic segmentation suggested that most of the youngest subjects would pass that task. Hence, even if the ability to segment syllabically were an early manifestation of the emergence of a general metalinguistic ability, the task would not be sensitive to this within the age range of our subjects.

3.2 Subjects

Twenty children were tested at each of five age levels: 4, 5, 6, 7, and 8 years. Half the children at each age were girls; half were boys. To increase homogeneity within age groups and heterogeneity between groups, all the 4-

year-olds were between the ages of 4-3 and 4-9; all the 5-year-olds were between 5-3 and 5-9, and so on.

All the 4-year-olds and most of the 5-year-olds were obtained from private
nursery schools, and were tested in rooms in their schools. The remainder of
the children were obtained from the kindergarten and first-, second-, and
third-grade classrooms of an elementary school, and were also tested in rooms
in the school. The elementary school was located in a neighborhood composed
mainly of white, middle- and upper-middle-class families. The nursery schools'
students came from essentially the same neighborhood and background. English
was the only language spoken in the children's homes. Written parental per-
mission was obtained prior to the testing of any child.

Data from an additional seven children were discarded. Two of these re-
fused to participate after the first session. Two others showed consistent
response biases on the comprehension task, one always choosing the top picture and the other the bottom picture. One child's data were discarded because he could not be induced to talk, responding to questions about the conservation tasks only with head nods and shakes. Another child's data were
discarded because on the synonymy task she responded in an apparently random
manner and overly quickly, often before the second sentence of a pair had
been read. And finally, one child's data were discarded when it was discovered
(after the conservation and comprehension tasks) that he had been referred
for evaluation for possible mental retardation. Five of the children whose
data were discarded were 4-year-olds; one was a 5-year-old; and the seventh
was a 7-year-old.

3.3 Procedure

The tasks were presented in this order: conservation, comprehension, synonymy,
acceptability, and phonemic segmentation. Pilot studies had indicated that
the conservation tasks were universally liked. They were presented first to
allow establishing rapport with the children quickly and easily. The comprehension task was presented next because the results from this task were needed
before the synonymy task could be administered. There seemed to be no compelling reason to order the remaining three tasks in any particular way, so the
order chosen was arbitrary.

The tasks were administered in a series of short sessions, the series
generally being completed for a child within the span of a week. Generally,
the conservation and comprehension tasks were completed within the first ses-

sion, the remaining tasks being completed in as many additional sessions as were required. If a child gave any hint of boredom or lack of interest in continuing a task, the session was discontinued. This was done even if discontinuation occurred in the middle of a task. That task was continued at the next session, after the child had been reminded of the instructions for that task. Testing sessions were arranged so as not to interfere with the children's school activities and were conducted only when the children (and their teachers) freely agreed.

Two experimenters each tested half of the boys and half of the girls at each age level. One experimenter was a male; the other was a female.

Chapter 4   A Study of Children's Metalinguistic Abilities: Results and Discussion

The results for each of the tasks, taken individually, will first be presented and discussed. Following this, the interrelationships among the children's performances on the several tasks will be considered.

4.1 Conservation

The set of conservation tasks used permitted quantitative scoring by, for example, allowing one point for a correct conserving response for each of the six tasks and a second point for an adequate explanation of the response. Cumulating scores in this way would yield a range of possible scores of 0-12. It is, however, highly questionable whether the scores obtained in this way would meet the assumptions of parametric statistical analyses. Conceiving of scores in the 0-12 ranges as reflecting an equal-interval scale would require, for example, assuming that an adequate explanation for one task is equivalent to a conserving response for another task, a dubious assumption at best.

For this reason, the conservation data were evaluated on a qualitative basis. Each child's performance was assigned to one of three categories: pre-conserving, transitional, or conserving. Children were considered to be pre-conservers if they gave zero or one conserving response but gave no adequate explanations. They were considered to be conservers if they gave conserving responses for all six tasks and also gave adequate explanations for at least five of six. Intermediate performances were classified as transitional. The numbers of children in these categories at each age level are presented in Table 4.1 where it is readily apparent that performance on the conservation tasks improved markedly with age.

The improvement in performance with increasing age was highly significant, $\chi^2(8) = 73.15$, $p < 0.001$. Performance did not vary significantly with any other variable — sex, experimenter, or task form. (All children received the same form of the Goldschmid-Bentler tasks; the task form variable refers to the

Table 4.1. Numbers of children at each age level at each level of performance on the conservation tasks

	Age in years					
	4	5	6	7	8	
Performance level						Total
Preconserving	16	7	3	0	0	26
Transitional	4	13	12	11	4	44
Conserving	0	0	5	9	16	30

forms of the comprehension, synonymy, and acceptability tasks which different children received. The nonsignificant result here indicates simply that the children assigned to different groups for those tasks did not differ in their conservation task performance.) Inspection of the data across these several variables yielded no suggestion of any complex patterning of the scores (i.e., interactions); for this reason no statistical analysis of interactions was undertaken. The only significant effect in the conservation task data was the one to be expected: performance improved with increasing age.

The reason for including the conservation tasks in the present study was, of course, to allow determining whether performance on the metalinguistic tasks was related to this measure of cognitive development. The most straight-forward way of determining this involves deriving from the set of conservation tasks a single summary measure of conservation performance for each child. Doing so, however, requires assuming that the six conservation tasks all measure the development of a single underlying capability, that is, that the tasks are homogeneous. The question of task homogeneity is of no small concern, for several studies have failed to find such homogeneity among various concrete operational tasks (e.g., BRAINE 1959; DODWELL 1960, 1962; TUDDENHAM 1971). Most directly to the point is a study by WINKELMANN (1974), who factor analyzed the performance of 5- to 8-year-old children on a set of conservation tasks similar to those used here. WINKELMANN's analysis yielded four orthogonal factors, suggesting a heterogeneity in the determinants of performance on different conservation tasks.

To explore the question of whether or not developmental changes in performance on the six conservation tasks could be regarded as reflecting a single underlying developmental change, two scalogram analyses (GUTTMAN 1947, 1950) were performed on the conservation task data. In the present context, a scalogram analysis can be viewed as a limited nonparametric equivalent to a factor analysis. To the extent that a set of tasks is scalable, the pattern of a subject's pass-fail performance is predictable from the number of tasks passed. Significant scalability indicates that all the tasks are measuring the same underlying variable and differ only in their difficulty (i.e., their pass-fail criteria). Such a result is equivalent to a one-factor solution in a factor analysis — both indicate that a single variable accounts for a major portion of the variance on all the tasks analysed.

The scalogram procedures developed by GREEN (1956) were employed. In both analyses, only the data from children who gave at least one conserving judgment but performed less than perfectly were included. Including the data from the others would have artifactually inflated estimates of the scalability of the tasks; the patterns of performance for children who passed or failed everything are, of course, perfectly predictable, but in a way that is unilluminating about scalability.

In the first analysis, only the judgment data were considered. A child was considered to have passed a conservation task if s/he gave a correct, conserving judgment on that task. The analysis yielded a coefficient of reproducibility $Rep_A = 0.900$, with a standard error of 0.019. The reproducibility to be expected had the tasks had their observed levels of pass-fail difficulty but been mutually independent (i.e., the minimal marginal reproducibility) was 0.715, yielding an index of consistency, $I = +0.649$. [I is equivalent to LOEVINGER's (1947) index of homogeneity; a value of $I > +0.50$ is generally considered to indicate that the tasks are scalable.] The difference between the obtained and the minimal marginal reproducibilities was highly significant, $z = 9.737$, $p < 0.001$, indicating that the major source of variance in performance on each of the conservation tasks is a source common to all.

The second scalogram was similar to the first, but included both the judgment and the explanation data. The results were also similar to those of the first analysis, yielding a slightly, though nonsignificantly, lower coefficient of reproducibility.

Thus, it appears that the conservation tasks used here are sufficiently homogeneous to allow deriving a single, overall index of performance for each child from the six tasks. The reason why the present results show greater homogeneity in the determinants of conservation task performance than did WINKELMANN's is not immediately obvious.

4.2 Comprehension

The comprehension task included two sentences of each of seven constructions. Numbers of correct responses, summed across sentence types, were subjected to a $5 \times 2 \times 2 \times 2$, Age × Sex × Experimenter × Task Form analysis of variance. Since the smallest cells contained data from either two or three subjects, an unweighted means analysis for unequal Ns was used.

The main effect for Age was highly significant, $F(4,60) = 20.01$, $p < 0.0001$, indicating an increase in comprehension performance with increasing age. The mean number of correct responses for the 4-year-olds was 9.54, while the mean for the 8-year-olds was 13.81. There was, in addition, a significant main effect for Sex, $F(1,60) = 8.79$, $p = 0.004$. Except among the 8-year-olds, where performance was essentially asymptotic, the girls performed better than the boys. Since no similar effect appeared for any of the other tasks, it is less than clear what should be made of this effect. Given the limited number and variety of sentences involves, it is perhaps best to avoid placing much weight on this sex difference.

The only interaction to reach significance was that for Experimenters × Task Forms, $F(1,60) = 4.60$, $p = 0.036$. Since neither of the main effects nor any of the other interactions involving these two variables even approached significance, it is unclear that this interaction is of any practical significance. No similar interaction appeared for any of the other tasks, so perhaps it is best regarded as an unimportant anomaly.

The comprehension task data were also examined in terms of performance on the several types of sentences. These data are presented in Table 4.2 in terms of the number of subjects at each age level who made one or more errors on the sentences of each type. Consistent with previous results, the data indicate that the passives and object clefts were more difficult than the subject clefts (and, presumably, also more difficult than actives). However, the present data, unlike those of SACK and BEILIN (1971), do not suggest that object clefts are more difficult than passives. Again, given the small numbers of sentences on which these results are based, it may be best not to make too much of such differences.

The data for the temporal relations sentences suggest that even the youngest subjects encountered little difficulty with sentences in which the events were mentioned in the same order in which they occurred and in which the propositions were conjoined with "before" (Type 1). The 4-year-olds appear to have had similar difficulties with the other three types. However, difficulty in comprehending "before" sentences that do not preserve the order of occurrence (Type 2) appears to have diminished earlier than for either kind of "after" sentence. The data thus appear to lend some support to the claim (CLARK 1971) that children understand "before" before they understand "after," even though they do not conform to the pattern of CLARK's data.

Table 4.2. Comprehension task: Numbers of children at each age level making at least one error for each sentence type

	Age in years					
	4	5	6	7	8	
Sentence type						Total
Passive	9	5	4	3	0	21
Subject cleft	5	1	1	0	0	7
Object cleft	8	6	4	4	1	23
Total of Ss making at least one error	13	10	8	5	1	37
Before, O.M.+	1	1	0	0	0	2
Before, O.M.-	10	3	1	0	0	14
After, O.M.+	11	9	6	4	2	32
After, O.M.-	13	12	9	3	1	38
Total of Ss making at least one error	16	15	12	4	2	49

The numbers of children at each level who did not understand these sentence constructions should be borne in mind when considering the synonymy task data, for they indicate the numbers of children who were not presented with sentence pairs involving those constructions in that task. For example, 49 of the 100 children were not tested for synonymy judgments on all of the possible pairs of temporal relations sentences, including two of the 8-year-olds. But whereas 18 of the 20 8-year-olds were tested on all possible temporal relations pairs, only four of the 4-year-olds were. In fact, five 4-year-olds failed three of the four temporal relations constructions on the comprehension task, as did one 5-year-old, and consequently received no temporal relations pairs at all on the synonymy task.

4.3 Synonymy

The synonymy data were first analyzed to determine whether the anticipated increase in correct judgments with increasing age occurred. For this purpose, the data were scored on a correct-incorrect basis, combining judgments of synonymous and nonsynonymous pairs across the several classes of sentence pairs, yielding a single %-correct score for each child. These scores were subjected to a 5 × 2 × 2 × 2, Age × Experimenter × Form × Sex analysis of variance using an unweighted means solution for unequal Ns.

The main effect for Age was highly significant, $F(4,60) = 12.12$, $p < 0.0001$, indicating that correct judgments increased markedly with increasing age. The only other main effect or interaction to reach significance was the main effect for Experimenter, $F(1,60) = 5.02$, $p = 0.029$. Since this variable did not enter into any interactions that even approached significance, this effect does not complicate the interpretation of the Age main effect.

To explore the nature of the Age effect further, a number of additional analyses were undertaken. Separate $5 \times 2 \times 2 \times 2 \times 2$, Age × Experimenter × Form × Sex × Pair Type analyses were performed on the data for each set of sentence pairs, such as the Active-Passive-Cleft set and the Existential set. Each set displayed the synonymy relationship in a different grammatical context; these analyses allowed determining if the age effect observed in the overall analysis held for each such context. The Pair Type variable refers to synonymous vs nonsynonymous pairs. For each set of sentence pairs, each child was assigned two proportion-correct scores, one for the synonymous pairs and one for the nonsynonymous pairs. Thus, Pair Type was a within-subject variable, the other variables being between-subject.

The results of the five analyses can be easily summarized. In each, the main effect for Age was highly significant (each $p < 0.001$). The main effect for Pair Type was also significant in each analysis ($p = 0.031$ for the Existential set; all other $ps < 0.001$). The Age × Pair Type interaction was significant for the Active-Passive-Cleft set ($p = 0.008$), approached significance for the Existential set ($p = 0.065$), and did not approach significance for the other three sets. No other main effect or interaction was significant in any of the analyses.

The nature of the Age and Pair Type effects can be seen in Fig.4.1, which presents the mean proportions correct for the nonsynonymous pairs (Fig.4.1a) and the synonymous pairs (Fig.4.1b) for each set at each age. Comparison of the two figures reveals that performance was consistently worse for synonymous pairs than for the corresponding nonsynonymous pairs, particularly for the younger children. The significant Age × Pair Type interaction for the Active-Passive-Cleft set appears to be attributable to the fact that there was no improvement with age for the nonsynonymous pairs of this set. The marginally significant interaction for the Existential set appears to be attributable to the fact that performance on the nonsynonymous pairs was asymptotic for the 6-, 7-, and 8-year-olds.

In attempting to understand the nature of the age trends, consider first the nonsynonymous pairs. The amount of improvement with age for these pairs was not very great. The greatest improvement was for the Temporal Relations pairs, for which the difference between the worst performance (the 6-year-olds') and the best (the 7- and 8-year-olds') was 20%. In addition, except

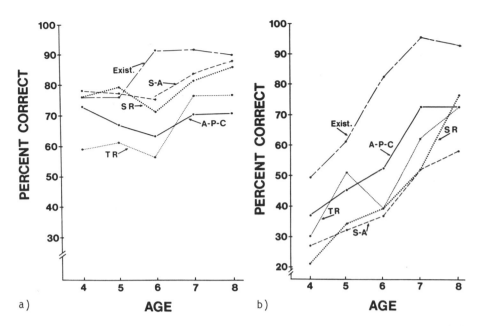

Fig. 4.1. Mean % correct responses on the synonymy task at each age level for each sentence pair type: a) nonsynonymous pairs; and b) synonymous sentence pairs. (See the text for characterizations of the sentence pair types.)

for the younger children's performance on the Temporal Relations pairs, performance was significantly better than chance for all ages and all sets.

There were, however, some substantial differences in correctness among the different sets of nonsynonymous pairs. The Active-Passive-Cleft and Temporal Relations pairs were judged less accurately at all ages than the other three sets; and there was a tendency for the Existential pairs to be judged more accurately even than the Spatial Relations and Size-Amounts pairs.

Most likely, these differences are attributable to differences in the difficulty of understanding and remembering the sentences in the different sets of pairs. That is, the synonymy task requires that the first sentence of a pair be understood and that its representation be retained while the second sentence of the pair is being understood. If children were unable to construct and retain representations of the two long enough to compare them, then their performance should be depressed toward chance. This possibility first became apparent when the materials for the synonymy task were being constructed. In checking the pairs to ensure that they were synonymous when they were intended to be and not when they were not, the experimenters found that many of the Temporal Relations pairs required very close attention. Sometimes it was necessary to read them more than once before it was possible to judge their synonymy. The problem was, essentially, that sometimes, by the time the second sentence of a pair had been read and understood, not enough could be recalled about the first sentence, particularly about the order of the events it mentioned, to be able to decide whether or not the two sentences were synonymous. At the other extreme, such memory problems never arose for the Existential pairs.

Upon first consideration, this account of the performance differences among the different sentence-pair sets appears to be inconsistent with the fact that the sentences the children judged in the synonymy task were ones which, on the basis of published data, pilot experiments, and the comprehension task, they should have been able to understand. But the synonymy task, involving as it does two sentences at a time, most likely imposes far greater (and perhaps qualitatively different) comprehension and memory demands than the usual picture-selection or acting-out comprehension task.

To the extent that the demands are different, comprehension tasks of the usual sorts cannot be used to evaluate the relative difficulty of the different kinds of sentence pairs in a synonymy task. What would be required is a task in which subjects heard a sentence, then heard a second, synonymous sentence (or a grammatically and substantively similar nonsynonymous sentence), and only then were asked for evidence of comprehension of the first sentence. Using such a task, particularly with children of the relevant ages, would be extremely difficult. Consequently, although the memory-load account of the differences between the sentence-pair sets is both intuitively plausible and probably correct, there seems to be no way of being able to evaluate it in any straightforward manner.

If this account of the differences among sentence-pair sets is correct, then the data would seem to suggest that even the youngest children were able to judge that two sentences were not synonymous *if* they could understand and retain the sentences well enough to compare them. This would suggest that it is comprehension and retention problems that cause performance on the nonsynonymous sentence pairs to be less than perfect. And it would suggest that it is an increase in the ability to comprehend and retain sentences that accounts for the (small) improvement in performance with increasing age. However, as will be seen when the data for the synonymous pairs are considered, there is an additional variable that affects performance on both synonymous and nonsynonymous pairs.

Differences between sentence pairs in comprehension and memory demands and changes with age in comprehension and memory abilities are clearly not sufficient to account for the children's performance on the synonymous pairs (see Fig.4.1b). The improvement with increasing age was far larger for these pairs than was that for the nonsynonymous pairs. Here the greatest improvement, which was for the Spatial Relations pairs, was an increase of 55%, more than twice the largest increase for any set of nonsynonymous pairs. In fact, the smallest improvement for a set of synonymous pairs (31% for the Size-Amount pairs) was larger than the largest improvement for any set of nonsynonymous pairs.

More important, however, is the fact that for the synonymous pairs (with the exception of the Existential pairs), the younger children performed *significantly worse than chance*. Any account that attributes improvement with age to an increasing ability to understand, retain, and compare pairs of sentences must claim that the worst possible performance is chance performance. Clearly, this account does not fit the younger children's performance on the synonymous pairs. Rather, they are doing something systematically wrong.

Consideration of what is required for making a correct synonymy judgment suggests an account of what the younger children were doing wrong. As suggested earlier, making this judgment requires constructing, retaining, and comparing representations of the meaning of two sentences, for they are synonymous only if these semantic representations are essentially identical. In addition, the judgment requires constructing, retaining, and comparing some kind of representations of the sentences' superficial forms, for only if these are different can the two sentences be synonymous. If the meanings and superficial forms are both identical, then the pair comprises two tokens of the same sentences rather than two different, but synonymous, sentences. Thus, deciding that two sentences are synonymous requires deciding that their meanings are the same *and* deciding that their superficial forms are not.

It is reasonable to suppose that a comparison of meanings will be more difficult to perform than a comparison of forms. Deciding that the meanings of two sentences are the same requires constructing representations of those meanings and retaining those representations long enough for the comparison to be executed. Further, it requires considering the meanings of the entire sentences, not just their parts. Deciding that the forms of two sentences are different requires only noticing that one contains a word or words that the other does not or that the words are arranged differently; it does not require understanding the sentences, nor does it require considering all of either sentence. Thus, the meaning comparison seems to be the more difficult of the two.

If this is the case, then there should be instances in which the form comparison was executed correctly but the meaning comparison was not. For nonsynonymous sentence pairs, the result would be the same as if both comparisons had been executed successfully: the difference in form for such pairs predicts the difference in meaning perfectly. But for synonymous sentence pairs, the outcome would be different. The successfully completed form comparison would indicate that the sentences were different but, because the meaning comparison was not completed successfully, the fact that the sentences had the same meaning would be missed. Thus, the sentences would be judged to be different, that is, nonsynonymous, a judgment that would be incorrect. Hence, judging on the basis of form alone would result in artifactually correct performance for nonsynonymous pairs and incorrect performance for synonymous ones.

This is, of course, just the result obtained for the younger children: their judgments of nonsynonymous pairs were correct significantly more often than chance, but their judgments of synonymous pairs were *in*correct significantly more often than chance. It seems likely that the reason for this pattern of results is that the younger children had difficulty performing both form and meaning comparisons on many sentence pairs and, consequently, often performed only the form comparisons. If this account is correct, then the major developmental change reflected in the synonymy data is that children become better able to make meaning comparisons. That is, the change is a change in the criterion on which children judge synonymy, a change from judging on the basis of form alone to judging on the basis of both form and meaning.

There are, then, two variables influencing performance on the synonymy task. First, there is a developmental increase in children's ability to take into account the meanings of a pair of sentences as well as their forms. This may be seen in the improvement with age from worse than chance to better than chance performance on the synonymous pairs. It also may be seen in the improvement with age on the nonsynonymous pairs. But the observed improvement for these latter pairs is less than the true improvement because some of the children's correct answers were arrived at on the basis of only a form comparison. That is, the children sometimes gave the right answer for the wrong reason. Thus, it is the performance change on the synonymous pairs that best reflects the developmental change.

The second variable affecting the children's performance is the differential difficulty of understanding and retaining the pertinent information about the different kinds of sentence pairs and, hence, the differential difficulty of making the necessary comparisons. The effect of this variable on performance on the nonsynonymous pairs had already been considered: greater difficulty yields performance at a level closer to chance but, with increasing age, performance improves for sentence pairs of all difficulty levels.

This second variable should also affect performance on the synonymous pairs, but here its effect should be more complex. Suppose, for example, that a particular pair was sufficiently difficult that neither the meaning nor the form comparison could be executed successfully. Performance should be at chance, for there would be no information available on which to base a judgment that the two either were or were not the same. A pair that was somewhat easier to understand, retain, and compare might allow a successful form comparison but not a successful meaning comparison. Performance should be worse on such a pair than on the more difficult pair (i.e., worse than chance rather than chance). A pair that was still easier to understand, retain, and compare might allow both form and meaning comparisons to be executed successfully, yielding better than chance performance. Thus, looked at across sentence pairs of differential difficulty, performance should be worst for pairs of intermediate difficulty, intermediate for pairs of greatest difficulty, and best for pairs of least difficulty. Looked at across age levels, performance for synonymous pairs of a given difficulty level should change from chance to worse than chance and, eventually, to better than chance.

The second of these predictions is difficult to evaluate for several reasons. Such changes with increasing age would, of course, be obscured in cross-sectional data by differences among children at the same age level, as well as by difficulty differences among sentence pairs within the same set and moment-to-moment fluctuations in children's memory and attention. And the initial portion of such a change (i.e., from performance at chance to performance at worse than chance) would probably not appear in the data by virtue of the fact that the children judged only pairs for which they could be expected to have at least rudimentary comprehension and retention abilities.

The first prediction, concerning differences between sentence-pair sets, is testable, however. The data for the nonsynonymous pairs suggest that the difficulty ordering of the sentence-pair sets is [Temporal Relations, Active-Passive-Cleft] > [Spatial Relations, Size-Amount] > [Existential]. Since for synonymous pairs performance should be worst on pairs of intermediate difficulty and best on pairs of least difficulty, performance should be worst for the Spatial Relations and Size-Amount pairs, intermediate for the Temporal Relations and Active-Passive-Cleft pairs, and best for the Existential pairs. As Fig.4.1b reveals, this is exactly the pattern obtained. Thus, the fine-grained pattern of the data lends some credence to the account proposed here.

The synonymy data obtained earlier by BEILIN and SPONTAK (1969) and SACK and BEILIN (1971) evidence much the same pattern we have discovered in the present data. BEILIN and SPONTAK found that nursery school, kindergarten, and first-grade children performed at worse than chance levels on synonymous active-passive pairs, but performed at better than chance levels on nonsynonymous active-reversed active pairs. A similar, though not as striking, difference in performance between synonymous and nonsynonymous pairs is evident in SACK and BEILIN's data for active-passive and subject cleft-object cleft pairs. In neither case is the performance of their youngest subjects on synonymous pairs as bad as was the performance of the youngest subjects in the present study. But in both cases the data represent a mixing of subjects who probably did not understand the sentences and, hence, probably performed at chance, with subjects who did understand the sentences but who, for the reasons suggested, performed at worse than chance.

To summarize, the major developmental change in synonymy judgments is a change in the criterion which children use. Initially, they can make neither form nor meaning comparisons. This is followed by judging on the basis of form alone, which in turn gives way to judging on the basis of both form and meaning. When these changes appear is modulated by the difficulty of the sentence pairs themselves.

The difficulty that the younger subjects apparently encountered in taking into account the sentences' meanings should probably not be taken as an inability to construct representations of sentences' meanings per se. Doing that is exactly what is involved in understanding the sentences. Published comprehension data, pilot data for the present study, and the comprehension pretest data suggest that that is not where the major part of their problem lies (see also SACK and BEILIN 1971). What appears to have caused the difficulty was retaining and comparing the semantic representations they were able to construct. For this reason, it appears that the development of the ability to judge synonymy correctly is separate from, and emerges later than, the development of the ability to understand sentences themselves. The latter is primarily the development of processes for analyzing heard sentences. The former involves the additional development of processes for retaining and comparing (i.e., synthesizing) the results of those analyses.

Thus, the emergence of the ability to judge synonymy in an adultlike manner appears to involve the development during middle childhood of a new kind of ability, an ability different from the comprehension abilities whose development began earlier and continues through this period. Conceptually, it is the comparison required by synonymy judgments that suggests a similarity to other, concrete operational abilities that develop during the same age period. That is, the comparison of the meaning of a sentence just heard with the meaning of a sentence heard earlier seems akin to the comparison of a representation of the post-transformation state of a conservation task display with a re-presentation of that display's pre-transformation state. Both require decentering attention from the most recent input to consider an earlier input and to reflect upon its relationship to that most recent input. It seems likely that the sentence-pair difficulty effects which modulate the children's performance represent the differential difficulty of applying an emerging cognitive ability — the ability to make mental comparisons — to materials of differential difficulty, a phenomenon much like the kind of horizontal décalage observed in the development of other kinds of cognitive performances.

4.4 Acceptability

The sentences in the acceptability task were constructed so as to be nondeviant or deviant in the ways described earlier. Initially, the experimenters evaluated the sentences' deviance against their own intuitions. To provide assurance that the classification of sentences as deviant or nondeviant was appropriate, acceptability judgments for the sentences were collected from two samples of undergraduate college students. The sentences were presented to one sample with instructions of the kind typically used with adults (see, e.g., DOWNEY and HAKES 1968). For the other sample, the instructions given the children in this study were used.

In general, the adult subjects' judgments agreed with the experimenters', though for many sentences their judgments were less than unanimous. There was no sentence initially classified as nondeviant that was not regarded as acceptable by a large majority of the adult subjects, and there was no sentence initially classified as deviant that was not judged to be unacceptable by a large majority of the adult subjects. There does, however, appear to be a relationship between the degree of agreement among the adults and the likelihood of the children regarding a sentence as acceptable or unacceptable.

Two findings emerged from the adult data that influenced the treatment of the children's data. The meaningful false sentences had been included in order to provide evidence about whether the children were judging on the basis of sentences' truth rather than their grammatical properties. Since (presumably) the only thing wrong with these sentences was that they were blatantly false, it was expected that adults, and also children who judged on the basis of grammatical properties, would regard them as acceptable. However, the adults did not behave as anticipated. Rather, the adults who judged them under the children's instructions tended to judge them unacceptable, a tendency that was somewhat less strongly evident in the data for the adults who judged under the "adult" instructions. It appears that adults who are looking for something wrong with a sentence will seize upon blatant falsity if there is nothing else wrong.

The adults' judgments made it clear that it would not be possible to infer from children's judging these sentences to be unacceptable that they were necessarily judging on a basis different from that of adults. Consequently, the meaningful false sentences were eliminated from all analyses of the children's acceptability data. Even so, the fact that the adults who judged under the children's instructions were somewhat more likely to judge these sentences as unacceptable than those who judged under the adult instructions causes some concern about the task as it was presented to the children. This concern will be considered after the children's data are presented.

The adults' data also indicated (as did comments made by some of the children) that one sentence intended to be deviant was not deviant for many subjects. Both adults and the children pointed out to us that "Yesterday Daddy painted the kitten," while perhaps not the kind of thing one *ought* to do, described something that *could* have happened, either intentionally or accidentally. They also pointed out that the sentence could be interpreted as an elliptical version of "Yesterday Daddy painted a picture of the kitten." Either way, the sentence was not deviant, at least not in the way intended, so it seemed best to eliminate the data for that sentence from consideration.

Eliminating that sentence required also eliminating its nondeviant counterpart from the other form. Having done that, balancing the two forms for equal numbers of deviant and nondeviant sentences required eliminating the other sentences in that category from each form. Thus, two sentences, one deviant and one nondeviant, which were described earlier as active subject-verb-object sentences with verbs requiring inanimate direct objects, were eliminated from each form. Combined with the elimination of the meaningful false sentences, this left a total of 28 sentences for each form, 14 deviant and 14 nondeviant.

Each child was assigned two scores representing the numbers of deviant and nondeviant sentences on which his/her judgments agreed with the adults' judgments. These scores were subjected to a $5 \times 2 \times 2 \times 2 \times 2$, Age $\times$ Experimenter $\times$ Form $\times$ Sex $\times$ Sentence Type (Deviant vs Nondeviant) analysis of variance. The first four variables were between subject, and the last was within subject.

The main effect for Age was highly significant, $F(4,60) = 32.61$, $p < 0.0001$, indicating that as age increased the children's judgments became increasingly like those of adults. The main effect for Sentence Type was also highly significant, $F(1,60) = 59.16$, $p < 0.0001$, indicating that the children were more likely to give incorrect judgments for deviant than for nondeviant sentences. That is, they tended to judge too many of the sentences to be acceptable.

The main effect for Experimenter was also significant, $F(1,60) = 19.00$, $p = 0.0001$, as was the main effect for Form, $F(1,60) = 9.08$, $p = 0.0004$. Only 2 of the 26 interactions were significant ($p \leq 0.05$), a number only marginally greater than would be expected by chance alone. Since inspection of the data suggested that the two significant interactions did not reflect interpretable effects or influence the interpretation of the main effects, they will not be considered further.

The significant main effect for Experimenter indicates simply that the children tested by one experimenter fairly consistently gave slightly more adultlike judgments than those tested by the other experimenter. The data offer no clues as to whether this was truly a difference between experimenters of the sort that might be expected if the two had administered the task in slightly different ways, or whether it was a difference between the children tested by the two. Consideration of the data for the other tasks does not resolve this question. However, the absence of interactions involving the Experimenter variable suggests that this effect does not compromise the interpretation of the other main effects.

The main effect for Form appears to reflect small differences in the extent to which the deviant and nondeviant sentences of the two forms were judged to be unacceptable and acceptable. As noted earlier, the adult subjects were less than unanimous in their judgments, and there were small differences among the sentences in the unanimity of their judgments. The Form effect in the children's data very likely reflects these same differences. Inspection of the children's data does suggest, however, that these effects were small and distributed across the sentences of the two forms rather than large differences which were localized on a few sentences. That is, there does not appear to be a pattern of differences between responses to the two forms that would complicate the interpretation of the Age and Sentence Type main effects.

The effects of major interest are those for Age and Sentence Type. These are presented graphically in Fig.4.2. For both deviant and nondeviant sentences, there are fairly consistent increases in correctness with age. At all ages, performance is better on the nondeviant than on the deviant sen-

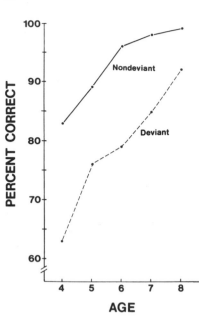

Fig. 4.2. Mean % correct judgments on the acceptability task at each age level for the deviant and the nondeviant sentences

tences. The difference is sufficiently large that for the nondeviant sentences the 6-, 7-, and 8-year-olds are all performing close to the asymptote, while not even the 8-year-olds have approached asymptote for the deviant sentences. Although the Age × Sentence Type interaction did not reach significance, $F(4,60) = 1.27$, $p = 0.29$, the improvement with age for the deviant sentences is far more impressive than that for the nondeviant sentences.

Overall, children at all ages were more likely to say that sentences were acceptable than that they were unacceptable. This is in contrast with results obtained by HOLLIDAY (1976) who reported that 5-, 6-, and 7-year-olds were biased toward saying that sentences were unacceptable ("silly"). The present data do not, however, reflect a simple response bias toward saying "right" or "good" rather than "wrong" or "silly." At all ages, the children were clearly responding differently to the deviant and nondeviant sentences. Furthermore, they responded differently to the different kinds of deviant and nondeviant sentences (see below). There may, however, be a component of response bias reflected in the data for the deviant sentences. It was only for sentences the children judged to be unacceptable that they were asked to explain their reasons. Some of the children, particularly younger ones, evidenced some dislike for having to give explanations. This may have led them occasionally to accept a sentence simply to avoid having to give an explanation. There was, however, no child who did this consistently throughout the task.

The fact that the children were more likely overall to judge sentences acceptable than unacceptable is reminiscent of the results obtained with younger children by GLEITMAN et al. (1972) and DE VILLIERS and DE VILLIERS (1972). But whereas the children in those studies were more likely to say that *deviant* sentences were acceptable than that they were unacceptable, even the youngest subjects here judged the deviant sentences unacceptable more often than not. Thus, the younger children's performance here is closer to that of adults than is the performance of the still younger children in those other studies.

Although the performance trends across age are similar for the deviant and nondeviant sentences, it appears that the two trends are attributable to somewhat different causes. Consider first the deviant sentences, for which the change with increasing age is an increase in the tendency to say that such sentences are not acceptable. This increase seems most likely to be mainly attributable to the children's increasing knowledge of the rules of the language — the constraints on how one can say what one wants to say. Essentially, the more such rules, or constraints, that the children know, the fewer strings of words they will accept as being consistent with those rules.

If the improvement with age in judging deviant sentences to be unacceptable results from learning additional grammatical constraints, then it should be the grosser, more obvious constraints that are acquired earlier. That is, there should be a relationship between the nature of a sentence's deviance and the time when children being judging that sentence as unacceptable. Seeking such a relationship is, however, problematic. As noted earlier, it is generally difficult to specify the nature of a sentence's deviance; this results in considerable uncertainty about what to seek in looking for such a relationship.

But, since the word-order-change sentences appear to involve violations of more than one rule, it does seem intuitively plausible that they are more obvious cases of deviance than are the sentences characterized as violating subcategorization rules or selectional restrictions. Figure 4.3 presents the age trends for these three classes of deviant sentences. It is readily apparent that the deviance of the word-order-change sentences is detected earlier than that of the other classes of sentences. Even the 5-year-olds are nearly unanimous in judging word-order changes to be unacceptable.

There are no consistent differences in the age trends for the subcategorization rule violations and the selectional restriction violations. This

78

appears to be inconsistent with the finding that adults judge the former to be less acceptable than the latter (DOWNEY and HAKES 1968). The difference between the child and adult data may result from the fact that a much more homogeneous set of deviant sentences was used in the adult research than was the case here.

Examination of the data for the several kinds of deviant sentences suggests that the developmental trends apparent in Fig.4.3 represent accumulations of several changes, each occurring at a different point in the age range sampled. For example, the data on selectional restriction violations indicate that there was no overall improvement for the 7-year-olds over the 6-year-olds, but there was a considerable improvement for the 8-year-olds over the 7-year-olds. A major contributor to this improvement is the "some"-"any" sentences. The 6-year-olds did reasonably well with many other kinds of selectional restriction violations, but had not yet mastered the complex rules governing the relationship between "some" and "any" and negation, judging these deviant sentences to be acceptable. For the 7-year-olds, the bulk of the errors on selectional restriction violations also occurred on the "some"-"any" sentences. The 8-year-olds, however, appear to have begun mastering the restrictions on "some" and "any," and performed considerably better on these deviant sentences than did the younger children. Similar changes appear at other ages for other kinds of selectional restriction violations

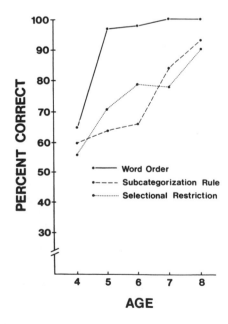

Fig. 4.3. Mean % correct judgments on the acceptability task for the different classes of deviant sentences

and also for various kinds of subcategorization rule violations. However, since the number of deviant sentences of any one kind was quite small, it would be hazardous to draw any strong conclusions about just when particular constraints are mastered.

The general picture which emerges, then, is that the improvement with age in judging deviant sentences involves an increase in children's knowledge of a number of constraints on sentence structure. Summing across a variety of deviant sentences yields the appearance of a smooth, continuous increase in the ability to judge deviant sentences to be unacceptable.

If this account of the improvement in the children's performance on deviant sentences is correct, there must clearly be a different account for their improvement on the nondeviant sentences. Not knowing the rules entails accepting deviant sentences; it does not entail not accepting nondeviant sentences. The fact that the 4- and 5-year-olds often judge nondeviant sentences to be unacceptable cannot be explained in terms of their not yet knowing the relevant grammatical rules.

In order to understand why performance on nondeviant sentences improves with age it is necessary to consider the explanations the children gave for judging sentences — both deviant and nondeviant — to be unacceptable. From a preliminary examination of the children's explanations and of those given by the adult subjects, it was possible to devise a system for categorizing different kinds of reasons for judging sentences to be unacceptable. The categories, together with examples from the children's data, are presented in Table 4.3.

Table 4.3. Acceptability task: Scoring categories for reasons

Category	Example sentence	Example of reason
1) No reason	The funny story read the teacher.	"Silly." ("Why?") "I don't know."
2) Denial of truth	Yesterday daddy painted the fence.	"Silly. Daddies don't paint fences, they paint walls."
3) Irrelevant or non-sensical	The playground walked to the store.	"No, the store walked to the playground. Stores and grocery stores — both of 'em — can walk, but not in this town — only on TV and cartoons."
4a) Possible negative consequences	The glass fell off the table.	"Bad." ("Why is that bad?") "Oh, his mommy will spank him if he breaks a glass. Sometimes I do that."
4b) Against societal rules	The boy hit.	"Bad, because you're not supposed to hit people."
5) Partially correct	The ashtray blew up the balloon.	"That's silly. An ashtray can't blow up a balloon unless someone threw it."
6) Correct by adult standards	The boy didn't have some cookies in his lunch.	"That's a little silly. You have to say 'any cookies' or maybe 'many cookies'."

Each of the children's explanations was scored independently by two judges who then discussed and resolved the discrepancies in their scores. It was frequently difficult to decide how a particular explanation should be classified, for the children were often less than articulate in giving reasons. For example, assigning a reason to Category 6 (Correct by Adult Standards) did not require the child to give the kind of explanation one might expect from a linguist. Such explanations were extremely rare, even for the sample of adult subjects. A Category 6 reason was often one that appeared to be of the same general sort as those given by the adults, with allowance made for the lesser fluency of the children. For example, if a reason given for judging "The string chased the kitten" to be unacceptable suggested that the child knew that only animate entities could engage in chasing (disallowing metaphorical extension), the explanation was assigned to Category 6. In many cases the category to which a reason was assigned represented an inference from what the child actually said to what s/he most likely meant. For this and other reasons, it would be unwise to place great reliance on quantitative comparisons of the frequencies with which different kinds of reasons occurred. Nonetheless, some general trends are clearly evident in the data.

Figure 4.4 presents the relative frequencies of different kinds of reasons given by children at different age levels. The most obvious trend is the increase with age in the frequencies of partially correct and correct reasons

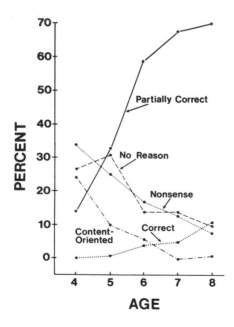

Fig. 4.4. Percentages of different kinds of reasons given in the acceptability task for judgments of unacceptability at each age level. (See the text and Table 4.3 for descriptions of the reasons categories)

(Categories 5 and 6). This trend, which is particularly striking between the ages of 4 and 6 years, undoubtedly reflects both an increase in the children's understanding of grammatical rules and an increase in the articulateness with which they could communicate their understanding. While it is hardly surprising that such a trend should exist, it is interesting that much of the increase in children's ability to verbalize adultlike reasons occurs before the age when they begin receiving formal instructions in school on such matters.

It is also not surprising that there should be a corresponding decrease in the frequency with which the children could give no reasons for their judgments or gave ones that were irrelevant or nonsensical (Categories 1 and 3). What is of greater interest is the decline with increasing age in the frequencies of reasons in Categories 2, 4a, and 4b. Reasons in these categories are all ones that can be characterized as "content oriented" in the sense that they involve an evaluation of the assertion made by a sentence rather than of the sentence itself. As indicated by the descriptions in Table 4.3, the younger children gave several different kinds of content-oriented reasons. Some indicated that they were evaluating sentences in terms of the potential consequences which the situations or actions described by the sentences might have. A judgment of unacceptability in this category suggests that the child deemed those consequences to be unacceptable. For example, several 4- and 5-year-olds judged the sentence "The big rock was in the middle of the road" to be unacceptable, giving reasons like "A car might run over it and get a flat tire" and "It would make a car go 'bump' and wake the baby."

Other reasons, similar to the "consequence" reasons, suggested that the children felt that the actions described by the sentences were things that one should not do — that they were things which, in the children's eyes, were morally reprehensible. Many of the younger children, for example, said that "The boy hit" was unacceptable, but not for the reasons given by the older children and adults. The older children said essentially that the sentence was incomplete (e.g., "He has to hit something"). The younger children, however, explained that hitting was a bad thing to do.

Still other reasons suggested that the children did not believe that the actions described by the sentences had happened or could happen. For example, in explaining why she thought "Yesterday daddy painted the fence" was unacceptable, one 4-year-old said, "Daddies don't paint fences; they paint walls." It is difficult to guess why she believed that; perhaps she had seen her daddy paint walls but not fences. In any event, it is clear that she was concerned with the actions daddies do and do not perform rather than with the properties of the sentence itself.

For some of the deviant sentences it is possible to see a progression from the content-oriented reasons of the younger children to the more adultlike linguistic reasons of the older children. Many of the 4-year-olds found "The boy didn't have some cookies in his lunch" to be acceptable. But for those who did not, the reasons were statements like "He *did* have cookies" and "That's not okay and that's not silly — what that is, is sad." Six-year-olds were also unlikely to give linguistic reasons for judging this sentence to be unacceptable, but their reasons tended to be different from and rather more sophisticated than those of the 4-year-olds. For example, one 6-year-old (who had judged the sentence to be acceptable) volunteered that it was "Okay, because maybe his mother forgot to put them in." His reasoning is certainly content oriented, but it considers that content in a broader context than was characteristic of the 4-year-olds. Many of the 8-year-olds also judged this sentence to be unacceptable, but their reasons were quite different from those of the younger children, such as "You have to say 'any cookies' or maybe 'many cookies'."

Approximately 24% of the reasons given by the 4-year-olds were content oriented. At first glance, this would seem to indicate that such reasons were not very frequent even for the youngest subjects. However, the only categories which attracted larger numbers of the 4-year-olds' reasons were No Reason and Irrelevant or Nonsensical. The extent of the younger children's difficulty in considering sentences per se is very likely underestimated by the proportion of their reasons that were classified as content oriented.

The Nonsensical or Irrelevant category was used as a "wastebasket" category for reasons that did not clearly belong elsewhere. It seems likely that some of the reasons tossed into this wastebasket were really content-oriented reasons that were too inexplicit or garbled to be classified as such. For example, the sentence "The playground walked to the store" elicited the following response (classified as nonsensical) from one 4-year-old: "No, the store walked to the playground. Stores and grocery stores — both of 'em — can walk, but not in this town — only on TV and cartoons." This could perhaps have been interpreted as a content-oriented reason concerning the kinds of activities in which stores can engage in some nonreal world, but it was difficult to make a strong argument for this interpretation.

Since nonsensical reasons were quite frequent for the younger children, such inadvertent misclassification may have led to underestimating the frequency of content-oriented reasons for those children. Since nonsensical rea-

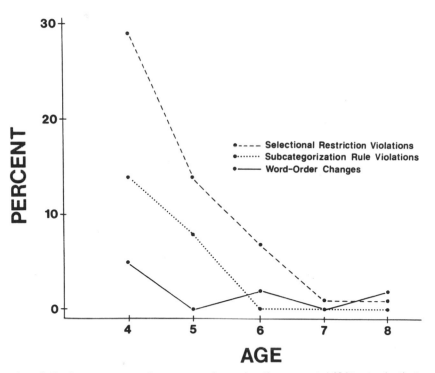

Fig. 4.5. Percentages of reasons given in the acceptability task that were content oriented at each age level for the different classes of deviant sentences

sons were rare for the older children, such misclassifications could have little effect on the conclusion that the older children do not give content-oriented reasons.

A second reason for tempering the conclusion that content-oriented reasons were not very frequent even for the younger children is that the incidence of such reasons was quite variable across sentences and across children. That this should be so is an inevitable consequence of the nature of the content-oriented reasons. Whether or not the assertion of a given sentence should strike a child as implausible or impossible clearly depends upon that child's knowledge and experience. More importantly, giving a content-oriented reason requires that the child has understood the sentence and has also found it unacceptable. Thus, many of the deviant sentences were unlikely to yield such reasons for even the youngest children: the nature of many of the deviations was such that the sentences were difficult, if not impossible, to understand in any way. Sentences that do not make assertions cannot be judged unacceptable for content-oriented reasons.

The deviations in the sentences violating subcategorization rules were often, though not always, grosser deviations in this sense than those in sentences violating selectional restrictions. Hence, the former should have been less likely to elicit content-oriented reasons for judgments of unacceptability than the latter. Similarly, word-order-change sentences should have elicited even fewer such reasons. As Fig.4.5 illustrates, this was the case.

In addition, the nature of content-oriented reasons suggests that they should be more common for nondeviant sentences than for deviant ones. The former do not violate any linguistic rules and, hence, if they are judged to be unacceptable, it should be for reasons other than linguistic ones. This is the case. Of the reasons given for judging nondeviant sentences unacceptable, 40% were content oriented; for deviant sentences, only 6% of the reasons were content oriented. The difference is highly significant, $\chi^2(1) =$ 110.99, $p < 0.0001$. In all of the other cases in which a nondeviant sentence was judged unacceptable, there was either no reason given or the reason was nonsensical. Since these cases were provided by the younger, less articulate children, it may be suspected that had they been able to give coherent reasons, those reasons would also have been content oriented.

It appears, then, that 4-year-olds, and to some extent 5-year-olds, are strongly disposed toward finding sentences unacceptable because of what they assert rather than because of the linguistic manner in which they convey that assertion. Whether still younger children would also show this disposition remains moot. Younger children have not been asked for their reasons for judging sentences to be unacceptable, nor have they been presented with the kinds of sentences likely to elicit content-oriented judgments and reasons. In any event, the tendency to judge on the basis of content decreases with increasing age to the point that the 7- and 8-year-old subjects in the present study never gave content-oriented reasons for rejecting the sentences that were presented except occasionally for the meaningfully false sentences.

The fact that the older children and the adult subjects tended to find meaningful false sentences unacceptable for content-oriented reasons suggests that this tendency never disappears completely. Most likely, there is a progressive decrease in the number and variety of sentences judged unacceptable because of their content. The younger children gave content-oriented judgments for a variety of grammatical sentences. The older children and adults did so only for sentences that were grammatical but also blatantly false, and even then did not do so all the time. Thus, judging on the basis of content comes to be reserved for sentences where there is obviously something very wrong but where there is no linguistic reasons for this.

Accompanying the developmental decrease in the tendency to judge on the basis of content is a corresponding increase in the tendency to judge on the basis of linguistic considerations. All of the interpretable reasons given by the 7- and 8-year-olds were of this sort. Essentially, the change is a change in the criteria used in judging — a decrease in the use of content-oriented criteria and an increase in the use of linguistic criteria.

It should not be thought, however, that 4-year-olds are wholly incapable of judging on linguistic criteria. The fact that they gave partially correct reasons 14% of the time indicates that even they could sometimes focus on the properties of the sentences per se. (Such reasons were generally given for rejecting deviant sentences, not for rejecting nondeviant sentences.) This early appearance of a very restricted application of an adultlike approach to the problem, followed by a gradual broadening of its applicability, is reminiscent of the horizontal décalages found in other domains.

Even though the 4-year-olds' reasons were unlike those of adults, their perspicacity was often striking. One 4-year-old, in response to the sentence, "The boy hit," was silent for a long time. Finally, the sentence was repeated, and he was asked, "Kevin, can Tubby (the elephant) say that?" He replied, "No," and when asked why, replied, "Because he's a *toy*!" In sum, the younger children were not approaching the task in a manner entirely different from that of the older children and of adults. But they only very occasionally used the linguistic criteria that the older children and adults used with considerable consistency.

To return to the question which opened the consideration of the children's reasons for their judgments of unacceptability, it appears that the reason for the age-related increase in correct judgments for nondeviant sentences lies in the tendency of the younger children to judge sentences on the basis of what they assert rather than the linguistic manner in which they do so. That is, the younger children judge some nondeviant sentences to be unacceptable because they are judging their content. As the tendency to judge on the basis of content diminishes, the number of correct judgments of the nondeviant sentences increases. The overall developmental picture, seen in the children's performance on both the deviant and nondeviant sentences, is an increasing ability to judge sentences themselves, apart from what they assert and also an increasing knowledge of the grammatical constraints of the adult language.

It might be suggested that the content-oriented reasons which have been interpreted here as evidence that younger children encounter difficulty in judging sentences per se arose because of the nature of the task and instructions and, hence, are artifactual. This would be, essentially, the argument that those children who gave content-oriented judgments and reasons *could* have judged linguistically but were misled by the instructions into believing that they should judge content. This appears to be the sort of argument that SCHOLL and RYAN (1975) intented when they objected to the DE VILLIERS' (1972) use of the terms "right" and "wrong" in their acceptability study. SCHOLL and RYAN argued that such terms might have encouraged the children to think about the sentences in terms of whether what they asserted was a wrong (i.e., morally reprehensible) thing to do. Thinking about whether something is morally reprehensible is, of course, thinking about content.

The distinction between, on the one hand, saying something in the wrong way and, on the other hand, saying something that is wrong (false) or describing something that is morally reprehensible is, to be sure, a fine distinction. But there are at least three reasons for discounting the argument that the content-oriented reasons obtained in the present study were artifacts of the instructions rather than reflections of the children's own criteria for judging acceptability.

First, the task instructions did not simply introduce terms like "right" and "wrong" (and "good" and "silly") without further specification. "Wrong" occurred in the context of describing the way in which the elephant talked, saying that he would "say it all the wrong way 'round." "Right" occurred in the context of the child's telling the elephant that he had "*said* it right" (emphasis added). Similarly, "good" and "silly" occurred in contexts that attempted to direct the child's attention to the way in which the elephant spoke rather than to what he said. Thus, the usage of the terms was quite different from what it would have been without such orienting contexts. The terms themselves, of course, are among those elicited by HOWE and HILLMAN (1973) from young children as descriptions of ungrammatical sentences.

A second reason resides in the nature of the results themselves. Content-oriented judgments and reasons came only from the younger children (except for the meaningfully false sentences). But the instructions were the same for all of the children and for one group of adults as well. If the occurrence of content-oriented reasons were an artifact of the instructions, why did the older children and adults not also give such reasons? If the instructions are constant and the performance varies, the reasons for the variance cannot lie in the instructions themselves. Rather, they most likely lie in the ways in which children at different ages interpreted the instructions. The fact that the older children and adults did not give content-oriented reasons is evidence that they could make the distinction between content and form. The

fact that the younger children did give content-oriented reasons is evidence
that they did not consistently make the distinction.

This does not argue, of course, that the younger children *could* not make
the distinction or that there are no circumstances under which they would not
give content-oriented reasons. There was, for example, no attempt made to
suppress such reasons when they occurred. There was not because it was felt
desirable to determine whether such reasons would occur. In addition, it is
considerably less than clear how they might have been suppressed. How, that
is, does one communicate the distinction between content and form to a child
who gives no indication of understanding that distinction? In any event, the
fact remains that the younger children *did not* make the distinction under
circumstances in which the older children did. At the least, that suggests
that the distinction is more difficult for the younger children than for the
older children.

Finally, there is evidence from other sources that 4- and 5-year-old children tend to respond to verbal inputs in terms of their content rather than
their form, for example, the experiments by PAPANDROPOULOU and SINCLAIR
(1974) and by MARKMAN (1976) that were discussed earlier. The tasks used in
those studies did not involve acceptability judgments. Therefore, the content-
oriented responses that occurred in those studies cannot be attributed to any
property of acceptability judging tasks. The difficulty that 4- and 5-year-
old children encounter in focusing on linguistic form rather than content is
a genuine phenomenon.

It appears then, that the development that is reflected in children's
acceptability judgments is basically a succession of criterion changes —
changes in the bases on which children make such judgments. Initially, there
is no real separation between what is understood and what is accepted. The
tendency to reject sentences that are difficult or impossible to understand
continues into adulthood, though the particular sentences rejected on this
basis change as comprehension abilities develop.

But whereas initially there is only a single criterion, later there are
multiple criteria. The change is not a substitution of one criterion for
another but, rather, an increase in the number of criteria. The present data
indicate that at least by the age of 4 years a second criterion has been
added — a content criterion. Children now reject some sentences that they
understand, rejecting them because they do not believe or do not like the
sentences' assertions.

Still later, an additional criterion — a linguistic criterion — is added.
Sentences continue to be rejected on grounds of incomprehensibility and fal-

sity, but these criteria come to play roles secondary to the linguistic criterion. By the age of 7 or 8 years, the majority of sentences that are rejected are rejected on linguistic grounds. Thus, 7- and 8-year-old children are judging acceptability on essentially the same bases as adults. The remaining errors for these children are attributable to their still being unfamiliar with some of the language's more subtle grammatical constraints.

4.5 Segmentation

The results for the segmentation task can be described rather more straightforwardly than those for either the synonymy or acceptability tasks. The main analysis treated the data in terms of the numbers of trials needed to reach criterion. As in the LIBERMAN et al. (1974) study, a criterion of six consecutive correct responses was used. Subjects who had not reached criterion by the end of the task were assigned a score one greater than the total number of trials (i.e., 43). Since failures to reach criterion occurred predominantly in the younger age groups, this had the conservative effect of underestimating the amount of improvement with increasing age. The means of trials to criterion for the several age groups are presented in Table 4.4.

The trials-to-criterion data were subjected to a $5 \times 2 \times 2 \times 2$, Age × Experimenter × Form × Sex analysis of variance. Here, as was the case for the conservation tasks, the Form variable refers to the forms of the acceptability and synonymy tasks the children received; there was only one form of the segmentation task. The only effects to reach significance were the main effect for Age, $F(4,80) = 35.96$, $p < 0.0001$, and the Age × Experimenter interaction, $F(4,80) = 4.30$, $p = 0.003$. The significant interaction indicates that among the younger children, those tested by one experimenter performed slightly better than those tested by the other experimenter; among the older children, the direction of this difference was reversed. The net effect is that the slope of the decrease in trials to criterion was slightly steeper for one group of children than for the other. But in both cases performance improved markedly with increasing age.

The effect of primary interest is, of course, that for Age. As expected, the nature of the effect is that trials to criterion decreased with increasing age. The older children were better able than the younger ones to discover that it was the phonemic structure of the syllables that determined the correct response.

Since learning to perform the task correctly involved discovering and using a principle, it is also appropriate to ask how many children at each age

Table 4.4. Segmentation task: Mean trials to criterion at each age level

Age	Mean No. of trials	% Children reaching criterion
4	42.10	10
5	36.95	30
6	24.90	85
7	19.05	95
8	12.05	100

level made the appropriate discovery. These data are also presented in Table 4.4. Few of the 4- or 5-year-olds solved the problem within the allotted 42 trials. Further, their performance during the task suggests that they would not have solved it had the task been extended indefinitely: there was no tendency for their errors to decline with increasing trials. It appears that the 4- and 5-year-olds were, by and large, unable to analyze the syllables into their phonemic segments and to count those segments.

The performance of the 7- and 8-year-olds was strikingly different. Only one (a 7-year-old) failed to reach criterion, and half reached it within 10 trials. In principle, the minimum number of trials to criterion should have been six. But during data collection it was discovered that the fourth item presented ("toy") was one for which many of the subjects (almost all were Texans) diphthongized the vowel to the point where it became two vowels. For them the correct response was that "toy" had three segments; for subjects who did not diphthongize so extremely it had only two. Since it could not easily be determined for an individual child whether the correct response should have been "two" or "three," children were considered to have reached criterion in the minimum number of trials if they responded correctly to the six items immediately following "toy." Hence, the minimum number of trials to criterion was 10.

Thus the data suggest that most of the younger subjects could not segment syllables phonemically. Further, the kind of instruction provided by the task — demonstration and feedback about performance — was notably ineffective in teaching them to do so. The older subjects were able to segment the syllables phonemically, and many of them demonstrated that they could discover the re- levance of the phonemic segmentation principal and use it correctly with only minimal instruction and practice. In this respect the present data accord well with those reported by LIBERMAN et al.

4.6 Relationships Among the Tasks

For each of the three metalinguistic tasks examined here — synonymy, acceptability, and phonemic segmentation — there were major changes in children's
performance between the ages of 4 and 8 years. Not surprisingly, there was
also a major change in the children's conservation task performance. The
question of interest now is whether the changes in performance on the metalinguistic tasks are all manifestations of a single, underlying development
of a general metalinguistic ability, or whether they are relatively independent changes that all happen to occur within the same general age period. In
addition, if the data indicate that the metalinguistic tasks are closely related, it may also be asked whether the underlying development common to them
is the same as the development underlying changes in conservation task performance.

For purposes of examining the relationships among the children's performances on the three metalinguistic tasks, the tasks were treated as involving
continuous, equal-interval variables. On the acceptability task, each child
was assigned a single score representing the number of deviant and nondeviant
sentences for which his/her judgment agreed with that of adults. The phonemic
segmentation scores used were the numbers of correct responses made during
the 42 trials. Scores for the synonymy task were arrived at by a rather more
circuitous route.

Recall that the synonymy task results indicated that children sometimes
arrived at correct responses for nonsynonymous pairs for the wrong reason,
judging them on the basis of their forms alone. Thus, the children's observed
performance on the nonsynonymous pairs was not an accurate indicator of their
true performance, combining truly correct responses with artifactually correct ones. For this reason, the synonymy task scores used in the correlational
analysis were the numbers of only the synonymous pairs for which the children
gave correct responses.

The correlations between synonymy and acceptability and between synonymy
and segmentation were both $r(98) = +0.60$, $p < 0.001$. The correlation between
acceptability and segmentation was $r(98) = +0.71$, $p < 0.001$. These correlations
indicate that a substantial amount of the variance in performance on each of
the three tasks is variance common to all three. The data thus lend support
to the hypothesis that there is a general metalinguistic ability developing
during middle childhood which underlies the development of adultlike synonymy
and acceptability judgments and the ability to segment syllables phonemically.

The magnitudes of the obtained correlations do not, of course, absolutely
compel this conclusion. It might, for example, be argued that the common var-

iance is sufficiently small that if there were a common developmental change reflected in the performances on the three tasks it is a relatively insignificant one. There are at least three reasons for discounting this argument.

First, the magnitudes of the intertask correlations must be limited by the reliabilities of the tasks themselves. The stability of the children's performances on the metalinguistic tasks is unknown. To have collected reliability data would have transformed an already large study into a gigantic one. Nonetheless, internal evidence from the children's performances suggests that the tasks' reliabilities were below the upper bound. On the acceptability task, for example, many children responded inconsistently to sentences which conceptually had the same status. And the sorts of memory and attention variations that affected performance on the synonymy task have already been noted. Since such variations undoubtedly occurred for individual children over time and sentence pairs, the reliability of the judgments must have been less than perfect. Thus, on statistical grounds the intertask correlations cannot be expected to be extremely high. Note, however, that the fact that the intertask correlations are high as they are indicates that the individual tasks were at least moderately reliable.

In addition, it is clear that the metalinguistic tasks do not yield pure measures of the development of a general metalinguistic ability. The synonymy data, for example, suggest that judging synonymy correctly also requires sufficient development of memory and attentional abilities to allow the child to have representations of two sentences available at the same time for purposes of comparison. And the data from the acceptability task suggest that performance changes there, in addition to reflecting an increased ability to judge sentences on a linguistic basis, also reflect increases in children's knowledge of the grammatical constraints on well-formed sentences. Such changes may be relatively independent of changes in general metalinguistic ability and also independent of each other. Hence, it seems reasonable that there should be components of variance for each task that are relatively specific to that task, as well as a common component. This, too, places a limitation on the magnitude of the correlations between tasks that might be expected.

Finally, the conclusion that the performance changes on the three metalinguistic tasks reflect a common developmental change does not rest on the empirically obtained correlations alone. In addition, it rests on the congruence of the empirical data with the conceptualization of the nature of metalinguistic abilities suggested earlier. In this respect, the *nature* of the developmental changes observed here plays an important role in supporting the conclusion of a common developmental change. That is, the performance change on each of the metalinguistic tasks seems to involve a change in the children's basis of responding — the sort of change that has been characterized as a criterion change. On the synonymy task, for example, the sequence of criterion changes appears to be from using no criterion consistently to using a form criterion and, subsequently, to using both form and meaning criteria. On the acceptability task, the sequence appears to be from judging exclusively on the basis of comprehensibility to judging on both comprehensibility and content and, then, to judging on comprehensibility, content, and syntactic and semantic well formedness. On the segmentation task the change is from not being able to segment phonemically to being able to do so. All these changes seem to be the sort one would expect to result from an increasing ability to deal with the language qua language and to be able to reflect upon its properties. If the relationships among the tasks did not make sense conceptually, the obtained intertask correlations would be less than completely convincing. As it is, they provide rather compelling evidence that there is some common denominator underlying performances on the several metalinguistic tasks.

Since it does appear that the three metalinguistic tasks tap a common ability, it can now be asked whether this ability is the same as that which underlies conserving performance on the conservation tasks. Here, however, the question cannot be approached in quite the same manner as was the question about the relationships among the metalinguistic tasks. The conservation tasks do not yield the kind of quantitative data required for analysis with product-moment correlational techniques. Consequently, to permit examining the relationships among performances on all four tasks, the data for each task were treated qualitatively.

The categories used for the conservation tasks were those described earlier: preconserving, transitional, and conserving (see p.61 for a description of the categorization criteria). The data for the phonemic segmentation task were dichotomized on the basis of whether or not a child met the criterion of six consecutive correct responses during the 42 trials.

As noted earlier, synonymy-task performance on the nonsynonymous pairs was not necessarily an accurate reflection of the children's true performance. For this reason, only performance on the synonymous pairs was considered. Judging synonymous pairs on the basis of form alone would yield a performance at worse than chance level. Similarly, if children consistently judged pairs on the basis of meaning as well as form (and did so accurately), their performance should have been significantly better than chance. Performances between these extremes could be attributable to a number of factors. But the most likely cause of overall chance performance is that some pairs were judged on the basis of both meaning and form while others, presumably the ones with greater memory and attentional demands, were judged on the basis of form alone. Thus, it seems reasonable to regard chance performance on the synonymous pairs as intermediate between the less advanced performance resulting from judging both meaning and form. (Note that this could allow misclassifying as intermediate some children whose judging abilities were so immature that they did not yet even judge form consistently; without any basis for judging consistently, such children should have responded essentially randomly.)

On the basis of this reasoning, performances on the synonymous pairs were assigned to three ordered categories: below chance, chance, and above chance. As there were 26 synonymous pairs, the confidence interval around $p = 0.50$ defined by $\alpha = 0.05$ is 8-18 correct responses. Scores of 0-7 were assigned to the first category, those of 8-18 to the second, and those of 19-26 to the third.

Categorization of the acceptability data also involved only a part of the data. Because errors on the nondeviant sentences were relatively infrequent and, thus, yielded relatively unreliable scores, only the judgments for the deviant sentences were used. Inspection of the data suggested that if a child gave the correct judgment for at leat 11 of the 13 deviant sentences it could reasonably be inferred that s/he was, overall, judging in an adultlike manner. The probability of this many correct responses occurring by chance alone is less than 0.05. Consequently, scores less than 11 were assigned to the lowest of three ordered categories. Scores of 11 or better were divided between two categories on the basis of the reasons accompanying the correct judgments. It was assumed, parallel to the assumption for many cognitive developmental tasks, that being able to give an appropriate reason for a correct judgment represented a higher level of competence than merely giving a correct judgment. Thus, the second category was composed of cases in which the child gave 11 or more correct judgments but did not consistently provide correct or partially correct reasons. The third category included cases where both the judgments and the reasons were correct for at least 11 of the deviant sentences.

In summary, the children's performances could be assigned to one of three ordered categories for the conservation, synonymy, and acceptability tasks and to one of two ordered categories for the segmentation task.

The contingency coefficient C (SIEGEL 1956) was used to evaluate the interrelationships between the categorized performances on each of the three meta-

Table 4.5. Relationships between the conservation tasks and the three meta-linguistic tasks (contingency coefficients)

	Synonymy	Acceptability	Segmentation
Conservation	0.53	0.47	0.52
Synonymy		0.38	0.39
Acceptability			0.33

linguistic tasks and performance on the conservation tasks. The resulting correlations are presented in Table 4.5. For completeness, the C correlations among the metalinguistic tasks are presented there also. All of the correlations involving the conservation tasks are significant beyond the 0.001 level, as is the correlation between synonymy and segmentation. The remaining correlations are significant at a level between 0.01 and 0.001. It is apparent that performance on each of the metalinguistic tasks is closely related to performance on the conservation tasks.

The C correlations among the three metalinguistic tasks are considerably lower than the r correlations among the same tasks. It should be borne in mind, however, that C, unlike other correlations, has an upper limit less than 1.00, the upper limit varying with the number of cells in the score matrix. For the C correlations involving the segmentation task, it is 0.717; for the others, it is 0.816. Even so, the fact that the C correlations among the metalinguistic tasks are considerably lower than the comparable r correlations suggests that the categorizations of the data for those tasks may have been less than optimal. To the extent that this is the case, the correlations between these tasks and the conservation tasks are probably also underestimates of the true relationships.

The significant correlations among the performances on the four tasks indicate that performance on each of the tasks is related to performance on each of the others, suggesting the existence of a common variable underlying performances on all four. It could, however, be argued that the source of variance common to two of the tasks was not the same as that between either of those tasks and the other two. Thus, to provide additional information on the extent to which performances on the four tasks reflect a common variable, a scalogram analysis was also performed. Here, as in the earlier analysis of the conservation task data, significant reproducibility would indicate that a single underlying variable accounted for a major portion of the variance in performance on all the tasks entering into the analysis.

The scalogram procedures developed by GREEN (1956) were used because of their applicability to non-dichotomous categorizations. The analysis yielded

Table 4.6. Difficulty levels of the tasks: Numbers of children passing each of the seven criteria

Criterion[a]	Number passing
Acceptability I	76
Synonymy I	72
Conservation I	67
Segmentation	63
Synonymy II	41
Conservation II	32
Acceptability II	26

[a]See the text (pp.92-93) for definitions of the criteria.

a coefficient of reproducibility Rep_A = 0.87, with a standard error of 0.017. The reproducibility to be expected if the tasks had had their observed difficulty levels but had been mutually independent (the minimal marginal reproducibility) is 0.66, yielding an index of consistency $I = +0.62$. The difference between the obtained and expected reproducibility coefficients is highly significant, $z = 12.41$, $p < 0.0001$, indicating that the major source of variance in performance on each of the tasks is a source common to all the tasks. That is, the performance changes on the several tasks are not independent changes that all happen to occur within the same age period. Rather, they are all reflections of the same underlying change.

The relative difficulty levels of the tasks are presented in Table 4.6. The differences between the numbers of children passing the different criteria are quite small in many cases. As differences in difficulty diminish, scalability becomes more difficult to obtain, suggesting one reason why the obtained coefficient of reproducibility is not even higher than it is. In addition, as noted earlier, the categorization criteria adopted for the metalinguistic tasks appear to have been less than optimal. To the extent that this is the case, the obtained coefficient of reproducibility underestimates that which might have been obtained. The other points raised earlier about the magnitudes of the relationships among the metalinguistic tasks, of course, also apply here.

In any event, the intent was not to attempt to maximize scalability by manipulating the classification criteria. It was, rather, to determine whether the developmental changes in the metalinguistic tasks could reasonably be viewed as reflecting the development of a single underlying metalinguistic ability and, further, whether this could be viewed as the same variable that underlies the developmental changes in the conservation tasks. The answer provided by the correlational and scalogram analyses is that they do reflect the development of a single ability. In this regard, the most compelling evidence is provided by the scalability of the data for the four tasks — a z as large as that yielded by the scalogram analysis simply does not occur very often.

Chapter 5   Reflections on Reflecting on Language

This monograph was opened with a consideration of the kinds of relationships that might hold between linguistic development and other aspects of
cognitive development through childhood. Cognitive-linguistic developmental
relationships during the sensory-motor period were considered only briefly.
One reason for this was that such relationships have received extensive discussion elsewhere, though without coming to any clear resolution of the issue.
Another reason was that the present research and discussion has been primarily concerned with developments occurring after the sensory-motor period.

It was suggested that the preoperational period is the occasion for major
developments in the abilities involved in producing and understanding language, the abilities most readily evident in the everyday use of language as
a vehicle for communication. The strategies that preoperational children are
developing for understanding languare are, it was suggested, of the same general character as the strategies such children are developing for interpreting other, nonlinguistic, inputs. This kind of heuristic strategy development,
although beginning during the preoperational period (if not earlier), appears
to continue well past the end of the period, perhaps continuing into adulthood.

Attention was then focused on middle childhood and a consideration of the
kinds of linguistic developments there that might parallel the cognitive developments characterizing the emergence of concrete operational cognitive
functioning. It was suggested that the parallel is to be found in the emergence of a set of new ways of dealing with language, ways that are different
from and require cognitive abilities going beyond those involved in understanding and producing utterances.

A review of the existing literature suggested that during middle childhood a wide variety of linguistic abilities — those characterized as metalinguistic — show striking development. Consideration of the psychological
abilities involved in metalinguistic performances of various kinds suggested
that they all involve controlled processing of sorts different from the more

automatic processing characteristic of comprehension and production. Metalinguistic performances, that is, require reflecting upon one or another aspect of language per se — in CAZDEN's (1975) terms, treating language as
opaque rather than as transparent.

The cognitive performances characteristic of the concrete operational period have, it was suggested, much the same character. In conservation tasks,
for example, the preoperational child has available only a set of heuristic
strategies for estimating the relevant properties of the arrays. The concrete
operational child, on the other hand, also has available alternative ways of
dealing with such properties. The availability of alternative approaches to
problems implies that a choice of approach is necessary, and choice is necessarily a controlled process. In addition, the decentration of attention that
allows considering the relationship between the pre-transformational state
of the arrays and their post-transformational state seems remarkably like
the "mental standing back from" an utterance involved in reflecting upon it.

Given the underlying conceptual similarities of superficially different
metalinguistic performances and also the similarities between their cognitive
requirements and those of concrete operational cognitive performances, it
was hypothesized that different metalinguistic performances would be developmentally related and, further, that their development would be related to
the development of concrete operational thought.

The empirical study reported here sought to examine the developments occurring between the ages of 4 and 8 years in three diverse metalinguistic
abilities — judging synonymy, judging acceptability, and segmenting syllables
phonemically. In addition, to allow evaluation of the hypothesized relationship between metalinguistic and cognitive performances, the same children
whose metalinguistic abilities were assessed were also administered a set of
six diverse conservation tasks.

The synonymy data suggested that at least a part of the developmental
change occurring during this period is a change in the criterion on which
children's judgments are based. Younger children tended to base their judgments on the superficial forms of the sentences, saying that sentences are
not synonymous if their forms differ even though their meanings may be the
same. Older children were better able to consider both meaning and form in
judging synonymy. This developmental change was, of course, modulated by the
character of the sentences being judged, such that sentences that were difficult to understand correctly and to remember did not yield correct synonymy
judgments as early as easier ones.

The acceptability data yielded similar suggestions of changes in the bases on which children judge. Evidence from other studies (e.g., DE VILLIERS and DE VILLIERS 1972; GLEITMAN et al. 1972) suggests that young children initially accept sentences they believe they understand, rejecting those that they do not. The present data suggest that by the age of 4 years children are tending to judge on the basis of the sentences' content, rejecting those that they do not believe to be true or that are descriptive of situations they find unacceptable. Even by this age, however, judgments are sometimes based on the sentences' linguistic properties. And, like younger children, 4- and 5-year-olds still judge some sentences to be unacceptable because they do not understand them. It is moot whether the content-oriented judgments characteristic of the 4- and 5-year-olds would also be found in still younger children, for such children have been asked to judge only a very limited variety of sentence types. The types they have been asked to judge seem intuitively unlikely to be ones that would elicit such judgments.

The developmental trend in acceptability judgments observed in the present study appears to reflect two different kinds of development. First, children come to accept fewer and fewer sentences that adults judge unacceptable, a change that most likely reflects an increasing familiarity with the rules of the adult grammar. Second, there is a marked developmental decrease in the tendency to judge sentences on the basis of their content, such that 7- and 8-year-olds (and adults as well) appear to invoke content criteria only for sentences that are linguistically well formed but have something very obviously wrong with them.

The phonemic segmentation task data obtained here were very similar to those obtained in other studies of children's ability to deal with the phonological properties of spoken inputs. Very few of the younger children were able to segment syllables on the basis of the numbers of phonemes they contained. Further, for those who could not, there was no improvement in performance over the course of the task, suggesting that their failure was attributable to an inability to deal with the phonological properties of the syllables rather than to a lack of familiarity with or understanding of the task per se. The majority of the older children, on the other hand, experienced relatively little difficulty in segmenting syllables and counting the numbers of phonemes they contained.

The results of the present study are, then, consistent with those of other studies of metalinguistic development during middle childhood in suggesting the existence during this period of marked changes in children's ability to focus on and deal explicitly with properties of language.

In addition to shedding light on the nature of the developmental changes in performance on each of the three metalinguistic tasks used, the present data also indicate that the changes in performance on the three were related. And this implies that these changes reflect a single underlying developmental change, the emergence of a *general* metalinguistic ability. There are, to be sure, undoubtedly factors contributing to the developmental performance changes on any one of the tasks that are unique to that task. Synonymy task performance was influenced, as noted earlier, by the difficulty of understanding and remembering the sentences to be judged, something that seems intuitively unlikely to be directly related to anything influencing performance on the segmentation task. But despite the existence of such task-specific influences on performance, it is clear that there is also a substantial common component underlying developmentally advanced performance on all three.

The present data also provide evidence of a relationship between performance on the three metalinguistic tasks and that on the conservation tasks. And this suggests that the general metalinguistic ability whose development underlies the emergence of developmentally advanced metalinguistic performances is the same ability as that whose development underlies the emergence of concrete operational thought.

To be sure, the exact nature of this common developmental change remains to be determined. It has been suggested here that is involves an increasing capacity to engage in controlled cognitive processing and, in particular, an increasing ability to stand back from a situation mentally and reflect upon it, whether that situation be an utterance to be evaluated, a conservation problem, or any of a limitless number of other situations. But whether the metalinguistic and cognitive ability that emerges is as general as has been implied here remains an open question.

The results of other studies of children's developing metalinguistic abilities certainly suggest that middle childhood is the occasion for a flowering of a wide variety of performances involving metalinguistic abilities — detecting ambiguities, appreciating linguistic jokes, discriminating rhymes from nonrhymes, and several others. If the common component in the development of metalinguistic abilities is as general as suggested here, one should expect there to be relationships among the developmental changes in all of these kinds of performances, and between those changes and the ones observed here, of the same sort as that found in the present study. It would, for this reason, have been highly desirable for the present study to have sampled metalinguistic performances more broadly than was done. But, as indicated earlier, doing so would have created a considerable risk of exceeding the limits on the children's attention and cooperation with the consequence of obtaining data that only poorly reflected their metalinguistic abilities.

By the same token, it remains to be determined whether the cognitive developmental changes that are related to the emergence of metalinguistic abilities are of the sort suggested here. The observed relationship between conservation task performance and metalinguistic performance is certainly suggestive, but no more than that. While changes in conservation task performance undoubtedly do reflect the sorts of changes characteristic of the emergence of concrete operational functioning, it seems unlikely that they are "pure" measures of such changes. And it is possible that they may not even be the best measures (see, e.g., LUNZER et al. 1976). Thus, it is conceivable that the obtained empirical relationship is attributable to something other than, or in addition to, changes in children's ability to engage in controlled cognitive processing, their ability to decenter, and the operational reversibility characteristic of concrete operations.

Determining this would, of course, require sampling children's performances on a far broader variety of tasks involving concrete operational cognitive abilities than the limited sampling of conservation tasks used in the present study. Again, it would have been desirable to have sampled more broadly in this domain here; but again, doing so was not feasible. Consequently, the conceptual and empirical analyses presented here do not more than suggest the possible nature and domain of the changes.

The focus here has been primarily on the nature of the changes during middle childhood in the character of children's linguistic and cognitive abilities, not on the reasons why such changes occur. As such, the characterization suggested here is essentially descriptive. Even if the suggestion that the change is basically an increase in the child's ability to engage in controlled information processing is correct, this in itself does not provide any account of the mechanisms underlying such a change. The same comments about descriptive as opposed to explanatory accounts can, of course, be made about Piaget's characterization of the transition from preoperational to concrete operational functioning and of most other formulations of the changes occurring during middle childhood. A discerning description may, nonetheless, be prelude to an explanation.

One reason for believing that the sort of characterization offered here of the nature and scope of the developmental changes may be apt is that it is not only consistent with the sorts of developmental changes in cognitive functioning that PIAGET and his followers have described, but, in addition, seems equally consistent with recent descriptions of contemporaneous changes in other domains. One obvious example is the changes that have recently been described in children's memory abilities during middle childhood. Here, too, development seems to be of two sorts, one a continuation of developments begun earlier, the other the emergence of a new kind of ability.

As FLAVELL and WELLMAN (1977) have pointed out, older children have more information available for retrieval than younger ones. Because they "know" more, new inputs are likely to be more meaningful and, hence, more memorable than was the case earlier. Implicit in this is that this sort of memory development is continuous and cumulative; and in this sense, it seems similar to the cumulative development of language comprehension and other inferential strategies that begins relatively early and continues into adulthood. The parallel is also suggested by FLAVELL and WELLMAN's characterization of these kinds of memory storage, retention, and retrieval processes as being ones that operate "unconsciously and automatically," a characterization suggested earlier as appropriate for comprehension processes.

It has, however, become increasingly clear in recent years that middle childhood is also a period marked by a different kind of memory development. Numerous studies have shown, for example, that during this period there is a substantial increase in children's use of mnemonic strategies for retention and retrieval (see, e.g., BROWN 1975, 1977; HAGEN et al. 1975). Employment of mnemonic strategies such as rehearsal seems to involve much the same kind of controlled, deliberate approach to problems of remembering as is evident in metalinguistic performances. Relevant here also is the finding by KEENEY et al. (1967) and others that younger children's failure to employ such mnemonic strategies results not from an inability to perform the necessary behaviors but, rather, from a failure to choose to do so. This is the deficiency that FLAVELL (1970) has referred to as a "production deficit" rather than a "mediation deficit" and, again, seems to imply that the pertinent development is of the ability to choose deliberately to engage in the task-appropriate behaviors.

Equally closely related are the developments during middle childhood involving children's knowledge and awareness of the properties of their own memories and of what may need to be done in order to remember something (see, e.g., KREUTZER et al. 1975; WELLMAN 1975). FLAVELL and WELLMAN's (1977) characterization of this as the development of "metamemory" indicates that they, too, see it as being a development similar in kind to that of metalinguistic abilities.

Unfortunately, the history of research and theorizing on the development of metamemory is at least as short as that of research on metalinguistic development. So there is as yet relatively little known about the character of metamemory development itself. And there is virtually no empirical evidence available concerning how metamemory development might be related to other aspects of cognitive or metalinguistic development (but see YUSSEN and BIRD 1979). But if the present suggestion about the existence and nature of a common denominator underlying the emergence of a broad spectrum of cognitive, memorial, and linguistic abilities during middle childhood is correct, such evidence should be forthcoming.

On first consideration, it might seem that the sort of view of metalinguistic development suggested here implies not only that performances on metalinguistic, concrete operational, and metamemorial tasks should be closely related, but also that such performances should *not* be closely related to other kinds of linguistic, cognitive, and memory developments. That is, if metalinguistic development is of a different kind from that underlying children's increasing language comprehension and production abilities, the former being related to concrete operational development and the latter to preoperational development, it would seem that the implication is that the development of metalinguistic abilities should be unrelated to the development of comprehension and production abilities.

When the empirical evidence is in, this may well be the case; but nothing proposed here requires it to be. It might be that children whose linguistic and cognitive development is more advanced than average during the preoperational period are also the ones whose metalinguistic and concrete operational development is also more advanced than average. Basically, this is a question about whether individual differences in the linguistic or cognitive developments characteristic of the preoperational period are related to those characteristic of the concrete operational period. As such, it is a question of a sort seldom raised in either the cognitive or linguistic developmental literature (but see McCALL et al. 1977 for discussion of a related question). It is, to be sure, a distinctly non-Piagetian question; but it is also one whose answer should have important implications for theories of cognitive and linguistic development.

There is one further aspect of the present research and discussion that requires comment, if only to avoid leaving the reader with an erroneous impression. The research presented here has concerned metalinguistic and cognitive changes occurring during *middle* childhood. Further, in attempting to characterize the nature of these changes, considerable reliance has been placed on phenomena and descriptions of sorts commonly associated with Piaget's stage theory of cognitive development. Taken together, these em-

phases might seem to suggest that the current view of metalinguistic development is that it, too, is a stage-related development, beginning only at the
point that PIAGET marks as the onset of the transition from preoperations to
concrete operations and being completed by the end of the concrete operational
stage. In the same vein, one might infer that metalinguistic development is
being conceived of as having the steplike character of a discontinuous, qualitative change of the sort often imputed to state theories of development.

The question of whether or not Piaget's state theory is really a theory
of discontinuous, qualitative changes, particularly in the sense of implying
temporal discontinuities, is moot (see BRAINERD 1978 and the following com-
mentaries). But however that argument is resolved, the present discussion
should not be taken as implying that children's metalinguistic abilities do
not begin to emerge until middle childhood or that they are complete and
adultlike by early adolescence. It was in the interests of avoiding this implication that the term "period" has been used throughout rather than "stage."

Such a view of metalinguistic development is already empirically untenable.
There is an abundance of evidence to indicate that metalinguistic development
begins quite early and some to suggest that it may continue at least into
adolescence. For example, the data from the GLEITMAN et al. (1972) and DE
VILLIERS and DE VILLIERS (1972) studies of acceptability judgments suggest
that at least as early as 2½ years children have some sensitivity to whether
or not they have understood utterances. That is, these children's judgments
seem to imply that they already have some rudimentary awareness of whether a
heard utterance has conveyed some meaning or none. A similar rudimentary
awareness of whether or not an utterance has conveyed meaning seems to be
implied by the observation (CLARK 1978; CLARK and ANDERSEN 1979) that quite
young children occasionally make spontaneous repairs to their own utterances.

In addition, CLARK (1978) has described a number of phenomena occurring
in 2- and 3-year-old children which she takes as indicating the beginnings
of an awareness of language in such children. SLOBIN (1978) has presented a
case study of his daughter which also suggests the existence of early rudimentary metalinguistic abilities. And although numerous studies have found
that children are not capable of dealing explicitly with the phonological
units in spoken utterances before the age of at least 4 or 5 years, LIBERMAN
et al. (1974) and others have found evidence of an earlier emerging ability
to deal with syllabic units.

These data, and others like them, suggest that the beginnings of children's
metalinguistic abilities can be found quite early in language development.
At the same time, it seems intuitively clear that children's early metalin-

guistic performances differ considerably from those of which they are capable later. It remains an unanswered question, however, how these early metalinguistic performances are similar to and different from those of older children and adults. The importance of this question lies in the fact that its answer should provide a characterization of the nature of metalinguistic development.

It is as yet far from clear how the similarities and differences between early and late metalinguistic performances might be characterized. There are, however, a few hints implicit in some of the discussions of children's metalinguistic performances that may serve to suggest what such a characterization may have to be like.

The obvious common thread running through discussions of early and late metalinguistic performances is that both involve some sort of "awareness" of one or another aspect of language. But a characterization of awareness itself is notoriously difficult, and nothing that has yet said about metalinguistic performances contributes to illuminating the nature of this common element.

There are, however, several ways in which early and late metalinguistic performances seem to differ. One characteristic of the early performances that seems evident in the discussions by CLARK, SLOBIN, and others is that they seem to arise rather spontaneously in the ongoing course of conversing. It is as if the young child, without particularly intending to do so, happens to notice and comment upon some aspect of an utterance. Certainly, such spontaneous noticings — that, for example, an utterance is incomprehensible — continue to occur as children grow older. As noted earlier, adults do much the same thing. But while adults are capable of other kinds of metalinguistic performances, it is not clear that young children are.

As the data presented here and elsewhere suggest, older children are becoming capable of more than these spontaneous noticings of properties of utterances. One way of characterizing this development is that they are developing the capability of *deliberately* reflecting upon particular properties of utterances. The difference here may be less one of the behaviors younger and older children produce than one of the kinds of occasions on which those behaviors occur. Suggestive of the difference here is that older children are becoming increasingly able to notice and comment upon a variety of properties of utterances *upon request*. Thus, one aspect of the developmental change may be that what can early occur only spontaneously can later both occur spontaneously and be done deliberately. This, of course, is exactly what one would expect if the underlying developmental change was, as suggested earlier, an increase in the ability to engage in controlled cognitive processing operations.

A particularly nice illustration of the nature of this change may be found in research on children's ability to deal with figurative language. As noted earlier, WINNER (1979; see also CHUKOVSKY 1963) sees some of the utterances of young children (i.e., 2- and 3-year-olds) as involving metaphoric extension. And NELSON et al. (1978) have suggested that some of the very early utterances that are generally treated as overextensions may have more the character of similies. That is, the 15-month-old who calls a horse "doggie" may, they suggest, not be misidentifying the horse as *being* a dog but, rather, noticing that the horse is *like* a dog, something that his/her linguistic capabilities are still too primitive to allow expressing explicitly.

Many of the examples presented of early figurative usages seem persuasive. But they seem also to have the character of being *spontaneous* usages. And it is considerably less than clear that the children who produce them *know* that they are producing figures of speech (i.e., that these are different from other utterances). This same point was suggested earlier in contrasting the early spontaneous "rhyming" behavior that WEIR (1962) and others have noted with children's later abilities to deal with rhymes.

The spontaneity of early figurative usages stands in contrast to the figurative language performances of older children (see GARDNER et al. 1978 for a review). Older children are becoming increasingly able to judge the appropriateness of metaphors, to explain them, and to create them deliberately (e.g., as completions for sentence fragments). In general, performance on tasks designed to assess such figurative language skills is quite poor until children are at least 5 years of age (though see GARDNER 1974; GENTNER 1977). Thus, the young child's ability to create figurative utterances spontaneously only later (and gradually) expands to include abilities such as judging, explaining and creating them deliberately.

Interestingly, GARDNER and his associates (e.g., GARDNER et al. 1975; GARDNER and LOHMAN 1975; WINNER et al. 1976) have suggested that the ability to interpret figurative language, and also sensitivity to variations in literary style, show major developmental changes during early adolescence. Further, they argued that these developments require formal operational cognitive abilities. As they have not yet reported data on figurative language capabilities and formal operational capabilities in the same sample of adolescents, it is not yet clear whether there is anything more than a rough temporal correspondence in the figurative and cognitive developments. If there is, then it would appear that the cognitive-linguistic developmental relationship explored here may continue well past middle childhood.

To return to the question of how early metalinguistic performances differ from later ones, it would appear that there is a second characteristic, related to the first, which also differentiates them. Although studies that have focused on children's early spontaneous metalinguistic performances have not considered the frequency with which they occur, it would appear that they are quite rare. The occasions on which older children and adults spontaneously make metalinguistic comments are, to be sure, probably also quite rare. But older children and adults clearly *can* make them more frequently if asked. And for some adults (e.g., those psycholinguists who make a habit of pointing out the ambiguities in others' speech or of deliberately misinterpreting such ambiguities), they occur quite frequently without provocation. Young children's frequency of metalinguistic performances is limited by their inability to engage in such performances deliberately, a limitation that is gradually relaxed as they mature.

Still a third difference between early and late metalinguistic performances that may be inferred from the available data is that there is much less variety in the aspects of language on which young children comment than is the case later. It may well be that it is only the most prominent features of language or the most glaring of errors that evoke such early spontaneous comments. It is, of course, less than clear what the term "prominent" means in this context. That, too, is a matter for further investigation.

In sum, then, what is proposed here is that the change in children's metalinguistic abilities is a change in the systematicity and variety of their performances and in the extent to which they can engage in such performances deliberately. Although metalinguistic performances may begin occurring nearly as early as utterances themselves do, these early performances are considerably different in a variety of ways from those of which children are becoming capable during middle childhood.

At this point, it may seem that more questions have been raised than have been answered. If so, that is all to the good. The intent was not to attempt to answer all the questions about metalinguistic development that one might think to ask. It was, rather, to attempt to provide some initial conceptual and empirical suggestions about what such questions might be and about the form that some of the answers might take. This goal will have been achieved if the present work stimulates research and theorizing on metalinguistic development and, particularly, on the relationships among metalinguistic and cognitive developments.

There has been a tendency — albeit an understandable one — for researchers to focus on one, or at most a few, aspects of cognitive or linguistic development, often leaving the impression that a great variety of independent and very different developments are occurring during the same developmental periods. The argument here has been, simply, that this fragmentation is more apparent than real, more in the data than in the child. Only by looking for relationships can one hope to find if they exist and, if so, what they are like.

References

Amidon, A., & Carey, P. Why five-year-olds cannot understand before and after. *Journal of Verbal Learning and Verbal Behavior*, 1972, 11, 417-423.

Bates, E., Benigni, L., Bretherton, I., Camaioni, L., & Volterra, V. From gesture to the first word: on cognitive and social prerequisites. In M. Lewis & L.A. Rosenbaum (Eds.), *Interaction, conversation, and the development of language*. New York: Wiley, 1977. Pp.247-307.

Bates, E., Camaioni, L., & Volterra, V. The acquisition of performatives prior to speech. *Merrill-Palmer Quarterly*, 1975, 21, 205-226.

Beilin, H. *Studies in the cognitive basis of language development*. New York: Academic Press, 1975.

Beilin, H., & Spontak, G. Active-passive transformations and operational reversibility. Paper presented at the Biennial Meetings of the Society for Research in Child Development, Santa Monica, California, March, 1969.

Berthoud-Papandropoulou, I. An experimental study of children's ideas about language. In A. Sinclair, R.J. Jarvella, & W.J.M. Levelt (Eds.), *The child's conception of language*. Berlin: Springer-Verlag, 1978. Pp.55-64.

Bever, T.G. The cognitive basis for linguistic structures. In J.R. Hayes (Ed.), *Cognition and the development of language*. New York: Wiley, 1970. Pp.279-362.

Bever, T.G., Mehler, J., & Epstein, J. What children do in spite of what they know. *Science*, 1968, 162, 921-924.

Billow, R.M. A cognitive developmental study of metaphor comprehension. *Developmental Psychology*, 1975, 11, 415-423.

Bohannon, J.N., III. The relationship between syntax discrimination and sentence imitation in children. *Child Development*, 1975, 46, 444-451.

Bohannon, J.N., III. Normal and scrambled grammar in discrimination, imitation, and comprehension. *Child Development*, 1976, 47, 669-681.

Braine, M.D.S. The ontogeny of certain logical operations: Piaget's formulation examined by nonverbal methods. *Psychological Monographs: General and Applied*, 1959, 73 (5, Whole No.475).

Brainerd, C.J. The stage question in cognitive-developmental theory. *The Behavioral and Brain Sciences*, 1978, 2, 173-213.

Brodzinsky, D.M. Children's comprehension and appreciation of verbal jokes in relation to conceptual tempo. *Child Development*, 1977, 48, 960-967.

Brown, A.L. The development of memory: knowing, knowing about knowing, and knowing how to know. In H.W. Reese (Ed.), *Advances in child development and behavior, Volume 10*. New York: Academic Press, 1975. Pp.103-152.

Brown, A.L. Knowing when, where and how to remember: a problem in metacognition. In R. Glaser (Ed.), *Advances in instructional psychology*. Hillsdale, N.J.: Lawrence Erlbaum Associates, 1977.

Brown, R. *A first language: the early stages*. Cambridge, Mass.: Harvard University Press, 1973.

Brown, R., & Bellugi, U. Three processes in the child's acquisition of syntax. *Harvard Educational Review*, 1964, 34, 133-151.

Bruner, J.S. The ontogenesis of speech acts. *Journal of Child Language*, 1975, 2, 1-20.

Bruner, J.S. Early social interaction and language acquisition. In H.R. Schaffer (Ed.), *Studies in mother-infant social interaction*. London: Academic Press, 1977. Pp.271-290.

Carey, S. *Less* may never mean 'more.' In R.N. Campbell & P.T. Smith (Eds.), *Recent advances in the psychology of language, Volume 4A*. New York: Plenum, 1978.

Carr, D.B. The development of young children's capacity to judge anomalous sentences. *Journal of Child Language*, 1979, 6, 227-242.

Cazden, C.B. *Child language and education*. New York: Holt, Rinehart & Winston, 1972.

Cazden, C.B. Play with language and metalinguistic awareness: one dimension of language experience. In C.B. Winsor (Ed.), *Dimensions of language experience*. New York: Agathon Press, 1975. Pp.3-19.

Chapman, R.S., & Kohn, L. Comprehension strategies in two- and three-year olds: animate agents or probable events? *Papers and Reports on Child Language Development* (Stanford University), 1977, No.13, 22-29.

Chomsky, C.S. *The acquisition of syntax in children from 5 to 10*. Cambridge, Mass.: M.I.T. Press, 1969.

Chomsky, N. *Aspects of the theory of syntax*. Cambridge, Mass.: M.I.T. Press, 1965.

Chukovsky, K. *From two to five*. Berkeley: University of California Press, 1963.

Clark, E.V. On the acquisition of the meaning of *before* and *after*. *Journal of Verbal Learning and Verbal Behavior*, 1971, 10, 266-275.

Clark, E.V. What's in a word? On the child's acquisition of semantics in his first language. In T.E. Moore (Ed.), *Cognitive development and the acquisition of language*. New York: Academic Press, 1973. Pp.65-110.

Clark, E.V. Strategies and the mapping problem in first language acquisition. In J. Macnamara (Ed.), *Language learning and thought*. New York: Academic Press, 1977. Pp.147-168.

Clark, E.V. Awareness of language: some evidence from what children say and do. In A. Sinclair, R.J. Jarvella, & W.J.M. Levelt (Eds.), *The child's conception of language*. Berlin: Springer-Verlag, 1978. Pp.17-43.

Clark, E.V., & Andersen, E.S. Spontaneous repairs: awareness in the process of acquiring language. *Papers and Reports on Child Language Development* (Stanford University), 1979, 16, 1-13.

Cometa, M.S., & Eson, M.E. Logical operations and metaphor interpretation: a Piagetian model. *Child Development*, 1978, 49, 649-659.

Corrigan, R. Cognitive correlates of language: differential criteria yield differential results. *Child Development*, 1979, 50, 617-631.

Cromer, R.F. "Children are nice to understand": surface structure clues for the recovery of a deep structure. *British Journal of Psychology*, 1970, 61, 397-408.

de Villiers, J.G., & de Villiers, P.A. Competence and performance in child language: are children really competent to judge? *Journal of Child Language*, 1974, 1, 11-22.

de Villiers, P.A., & de Villiers, J.G. Early judgments of semantic and syntactic acceptability by children. *Journal of Psycholinguistic Research*, 1972, 1, 299-310.

Dodwell, P.C. Children's understanding of number and related concepts. *Canadian Journal of Psychology*, 1960, 14, 191-205.

Dodwell, P.C. Relations between the understanding of the logic of classes and of cardinal number in children. *Canadian Journal of Psychology*, 1962, 16, 152-160.

Donaldson, M., & Balfour, G. Less is more. A study of language comprehension in children. *British Journal of Psychology*, 1968, 59, 461-471.

Dore, J. A pragmatic description of early language development. *Journal of Psycholinguistic Research*, 1974, 3, 343-350.

Dore, J. Holophrases, speech acts and language universals. *Journal of Child Language*, 1975, 2, 21-40.

Downey, R.G., & Hakes, D.T. Some psychological effects of violating linguistic rules. *Journal of Verbal Learning and Verbal Behavior*, 1968, 7, 158-161.

Downing, J., & Oliver, P. The child's conception of a word. *Reading Research Quarterly*, 1973-74, 9, 568-582.

Edwards, D. Sensory-motor intelligence and semantic relations in early child grammar. *Cognition*, 1973, 2, 395-434.

Eilers, R.E., Oller, D.K., & Ellington, J. The acquisition of wordmeaning for dimensional adjectives: the long and short of it. *Journal of Child Language*, 1974, 1, 195-204.

Evans, J.S. Children's comprehension and processing of ambiguous words in sentences. Unpublished Ph.D. dissertation, The University of Texas at Austin, 1976.

Ferguson, C.A., & Slobin, D.I. (Eds.) *Studies of child language development.* New York: Holt, Rinehart and Winston, 1973.

Flavell, J.H. Developmental studies of mediated memory. In H.W. Reese & L.P. Lipsitt (Eds.), *Advances in child development and behavior, Volume 5.* New York: Academic Press, 1970.

Flavell, J.H. *Cognitive development.* Englewood Cliffs, N.J.: Prentice-Hall, 1977.

Flavell, J.H., & Wellman, H.W. Metamemory. In R.V. Kail, Jr., & J.W. Hagen (Eds.), *Perspectives on the development of memory and cognition.* Hillsdale, N.J.: Lawrence Erlbaum Associates, 1977. Pp.3-33.

Foss, D.J. Some effects of ambiguity upon sentence comprehension. *Journal of Verbal Learning and Verbal Behavior*, 1970, 9, 699-706.

Foss, D.J., & Hakes, D.T. *Psycholinguistics: an introduction to the psychology of language.* Englewood Cliffs, N.J.: Prentice-Hall, 1978.

Foss, D.J., & Jenkins, C.M. Some effects of context on the comprehension of ambiguous sentences. *Journal of Verbal Learning and Verbal Behavior*, 1973, 12, 577-589.

Foss, D.J., & Swinney, D.A. On the psychological reality of the phoneme: perception, identification, and consciousness. *Journal of Verbal Learning and Verbal Behavior*, 1973, 12, 246-257.

Fowles, B., & Glanz, M.E. Competence and talent in verbal riddle comprehension. *Journal of Child Language*, 1977, 4, 433-452.

Fox, B., & Routh, D.K. Analyzing spoken language into words, syllables, and phonemes: a developmental study. *Journal of Psycholinguistic Research*, 1975, 4, 331-342.

Fox, B., & Routh, D.K. Phonemic analysis and synthesis as word-attack skills. *Journal of Educational Psychology*, 1976, 68, 70-74.

Gardner, H. Metaphors and modalities: how children project polar adjectives onto diverse domains. *Child Development*, 1974, 45, 84-91.

Gardner, H., Kircher, M., Winner, E., & Perkins, D. Children's metaphoric productions and preferences. *Journal of Child Language*, 1975, 2, 135-141.

Gardner, H., & Lohman, W. Children's sensitivity to literary styles. *Merrill-Palmer Quarterly*, 1975, 21, 113-126.

Gardner, H., Winner, E., Bechhofer, R., & Wolf, D. The development of figurative language. In K.E. Nelson (Ed.), *Children's language, Volume 1.* New York: Gardner Press, 1978.

Garnica, O.K. The development of phonemic speech perception. In T.E. Moore (Ed.), *Cognitive development and the acquisition of language.* New York: Academic Press, 1973. Pp.215-222.

Gelman, R., & Gallistel, C.R. *The child's understanding of number.* Cambridge, Mass.: Harvard University Press, 1978.

Gentner, D. If a tree had a knee, where would it be? Children's performance on simple spatial metaphors. *Papers and Reports on Child Language Development* (Stanford University), 1977, 13, 157-164.

Gleitman, L.R. Linguistic awareness and reading. Paper presented at the Interdisciplinary Institute on Child Development and Reading, Newark, Delaware, 1974.

Gleitman, L.R., Gleitman, H., & Shipley, E.F. The emergence of the child as grammarian. *Cognition*, 1972, 1, 137-164.

Gleitman, L.R., & Rozin, P. Teaching reading by use of a syllabary. *Reading Research Quarterly*, 1973, 8, 447-483.

Goldschmid, M.L., & Bentler, P.M. *Instruction manual — Concept Assessment Kit: Conservation*. San Diego: Educational and Industrial Testing Service, 1968.

Gowie, C.J., & Powers, J.E. Children's use of expectations as a source of information in language comprehension. *Journal of Experimental Child Psychology*, 1978, 26, 472-488.

Green, B.F. A method of scalogram analysis using summary statistics. *Psychometrika*, 1956, 21, 79-88.

Greenfield, P.M., & Smith, J.H. *The structure of communication in early language development*. New York: Academic Press, 1976.

Guttman, L. The Cornell technique for scale and intensity analysis. *Educational and Psychological Measurement*, 1947, 7, 247-279.

Guttman, L. The basis for scalogram analysis. In S.A. Stouffer et al., *Measurement and prediction*. Princeton, N.J.: Princeton University Press, 1950. Pp.60-90.

Hagen, J.W., Jongeward, R.H., Jr., & Kail, R.V., Jr. Cognitive perspectives on the development of memory. In H.W. Reese (Ed.), *Advances in child development, Volume 10*. New York: Academic Press, 1975. Pp.57-103.

Hirsh-Pasek, K., Gleitman, L.R., & Gleitman, H. What does the brain say to the mind? A study of the detection and report of ambiguity by young children. In A. Sinclair, R.J. Jarvella, & W.J.M. Levelt (Eds.), *The child's conception of language*. Berlin: Springer-Verlag, 1978. Pp.97-132.

Holden, M.H., & MacGinitie, W.H. Children's conceptions of word boundaries in speech and print. *Journal of Educational Psychology*, 1972, 63, 551-557.

Holliday, J. Response bias in children's judgments of sense of sentences. *Perceptual and Motor Skills*, 1976, 43, 660-662.

Howe, H.E., Jr., & Hillman, D. The acquisition of semantic restrictions in children. *Journal of Verbal Learning and Verbal Behavior*, 1973, 12, 132-139.

James, S.L., & Miller, J.F. Children's awareness of semantic constraints in sentences. *Child Development*, 1973, 44, 69-76.

Jusczyk, P.W. Rhymes and reasons: some aspects of the child's appreciation of poetic form. *Developmental Psychology*, 1977, 13, 599-607.

Keeney, T.J., Cannizzo, S.R., & Flavell, J.H. Spontaneous and induced verbal rehearsal in a recall task. *Child Development*, 1967, 38, 953-966.

Kemler, D.G., & Smith, L.B. Is there a developmental trend from integrality to separability in perception? *Journal of Experimental Child Psychology*, 1978, 26, 498-507.

Kessel, F.S. The role of syntax in children's comprehension from ages six to twelve. *Monographs of the Society for Research in Child Development*, 1970, 35 (6, Serial No.139).

Klima, E.S., & Bellugi, U. Syntactic regularities in the speech of children. In J. Lyons & R.C. Wales (Eds.), *Psycholinguistic papers: the proceedings of the 1966 Edinburgh Conference*. Edinburgh: Edinburgh University Press, 1966. Pp.183-208.

Knafle, J.D. Children's discrimination of rhyme. *Journal of Speech and Hearing Research*, 1974, 17, 367-372.

Kramer, P.E., Koff, E., & Luria, Z. The development of competence in an exceptional language structure in older children and young adults. *Child Development*, 1972, 43, 121-130.

Kreutzer, M.A., Leonard, C., & Flavell, J.H. An interview study of children's knowledge about memory. *Monographs of the Society for Research in Child Development*, 1975, 40 (1, Serial No.159).

Kuczaj, S.A., II, & Maratsos, M.P. On the acquisition of *front*, *back*, and *side*. *Child Development*, 1975, 46, 202-210.

LaBerge, D., & Samuels, S.J. Toward a theory of automatic information processing in reading. *Cognitive Psychology*, 1974, 6, 293-323.

LaPointe, K., & O'Donnell, J.P. Number conservation in children below age six: its relationship to age, perceptual dimensions, and language comprehension. *Developmental Psychology*, 1974, 10, 422-428.

Liberman, A.M., Cooper, F.S., Shankweiler, D.P., & Studdert-Kennedy, M. Perception of the speech code. *Psychological Review*, 1967, 74, 431-461.

Liberman, I.Y., Shankweiler, D., Fischer, F.W., & Carter, B. Explicit syllable and phoneme segmentation in the young child. *Journal of Experimental Child Psychology*, 1974, 18, 201-212.

Liberman, I.Y., Shankweiler, D., Liberman, A.M., Fowler, C., & Fischer, F.W. Phonetic segmentation and recoding in the beginning reader. In A.S. Reber & D.L. Scarborough (Eds.), *Toward a psychology of reading*. Hillsdale, N.J.: Lawrence Erlbaum Associates, 1977. Pp.207-226.

Loevinger, J. A systematic approach to the construction and evaluation of tests of ability. *Psychological Monographs*, 1947, 61, No.4.

Lumsden, E.A., Jr., & Poteat, B.W. The salience of the vertical dimension in the concept of "bigger" in five- and six-year olds. *Journal of Verbal Learning and Verbal Behavior*, 1968, 7, 404-408.

Lungberg, I., & Torneus, M. Nonreaders awareness of the basic relationship between spoken and written words. *Journal of Experimental Child Psychology*, 1978, 25, 404-412.

Lunzer, E.A., Dolan, T., & Wilkinson, J.E. The effectiveness of measures of operativity, language and short-term memory in the prediction of reading and mathematical understanding. *British Journal of Educational Psychology*, 1976, 46, 295-305.

Lunzer, E.A., Wilkinson, J.E., & Dolan, T. The distinctiveness of operativity as a measure of cognitive functioning in five year old children. *British Journal of Educational Psychology*, 1976, 46, 280-294.

Macnamara, J. Cognitive basis of language learning in infants. *Psychological Review*, 1972, 79, 1-13.

Macnamara, J. From sign to language. In J. Macnamara (Ed.), *Language learning and thought*. New York: Academic Press, 1977. Pp.11-35.

Maratsos, M.P. Decrease in the understanding of the word "big" in preschool children. *Child Development*, 1973, 44, 747-752.

Maratsos, M.P. When is a high thing the big one? *Developmental Psychology*, 1974, 10, 367-375. (a)

Maratsos, M.P. How preschool children understand missing complement subjects. *Child Development*, 1974, 45, 700-706. (b)

Markman, E.M. Children's difficulty with word-reference differentiation. *Child Development*, 1976, 47, 742-749.

McCall, R.B., Eichorn, D.H., & Hogarty, P.S. Transitions in early mental development. *Monographs of the Society for Research in Child Development*, 1977, 42 (3, Serial No.171).

McGhee, P.E. Cognitive mastery and children's humor. *Psychological Bulletin*, 1974, 81, 721-730.

McGhee, P.E. A model of the origins and early development of incongruity-based humour. In A.J. Chapman & H.C. Foot (Eds.), *It's a funny thing, humour*. Oxford: Pergamon Press, 1977.

Moerk, E.L. Piaget's research as applied to an explanation of language development. *Merrill-Palmer Quarterly*, 1975, 21, 151-169.

Nelson, K., Rescorla, L., Gruendel, J., & Benedict, H. Early lexicons: what do they mean? *Child Development*, 1978, 49, 960-968.

Palermo, D.S. More about less: a study of language comprehension. *Journal of Verbal Learning and Verbal Behavior*, 1973, 12, 211-221.

Palermo, D.S. Still more about the comprehension of 'less'. *Developmental Psychology*, 1974, 10, 827-829.

Papandropoulou, I., & Sinclair, H. What is a word? Experimental study of children's idea on grammar. *Human Development*, 1974, 17, 241-258.

Piaget, J. *The grasp of consciousness: action and concept in the young child*. Cambridge, Mass.: Harvard University Press, 1976.

Piaget, J. *Success and understanding*. Cambridge, Mass.: Harvard University Press, 1978.

Pufall, P.B., & Shaw, R.E. Precocious thoughts on number: the long and short of it. *Developmental Psychology*, 1972, 7, 62-69.

Rozin, P., Bressman, B., & Taft, M. Do children understand the basic relationship between speech and writing? The mow-motorcycle test. *Journal of Reading Behavior*, 1974, 6, 327-334.

Sack, H.G., & Beilin, H. Meaning equivalence of active-passive and subject-object first cleft sentences. Paper presented at the Developmental Psycholinguistics Conference, State University of New York at Buffalo, New York, 1971.

Savin, H.B. What the child knows about speech when he starts to learn to read. In J.F. Kavanagh & I.G. Mattingly (Eds.), *Language by ear and by eye: the relationships between speech and reading*. Cambridge, Mass.: M.I.T. Press, 1972. Pp.319-326.

Savin, H.B., & Bever, T.G. The nonperceptual reality of the phoneme. *Journal of Verbal Learning and Verbal Behavior*, 1970, 9, 295-302.

Schneider, W., & Shiffrin, R.M. Controlled and automatic human information processing: I. Detection, search, and attention. *Psychological Review*, 1977, 84, 1-66.

Scholl, D.M., & Ryan, E.B. Child judgments of sentences varying in grammatical complexity. *Journal of Experimental Child Psychology*, 1975, 20, 274-285.

Scholnick, E.K., & Adams, M.J. Relationships between language and cognitive skills: passive-voice comprehension, backward repetition, and matrix permutation. *Child Development*, 1973, 44, 741-746.

Shepp, B.E. From perceived similarity to dimensional structure. In E. Rosch & B. Lloyd (Eds.), *On the nature and principle of formation of categories*. Hillsdale, N.J.: Lawrence Erlbaum Associates, 1978.

Shiffrin, R.M., & Schneider, W. Controlled and automatic human information processing: II. Perceptual learning, automatic attending, and a general theory. *Psychological Review*, 1977, 84, 127-190.

Shultz, T.R. A cognitive-developmental analysis of humor. In A.J. Chapman & H.C. Foote (Eds.), *Humour and laughter: theory, research, and applications*. London: Wiley, 1976. Pp.11-36.

Shultz, T.R., & Horibe, F. Development of the appreciation of verbal jokes. *Developmental Psychology*, 1974, 10, 13-20.

Shultz, T.R., & Pilon, R. Development of the ability to detect linguistic ambiguity. *Child Development*, 1973, 44, 728-733.

Shvachkin, N.Kh. The development of phonemic speech perception in early childhood. In C.A. Ferguson & D.I. Slobin (Eds.), *Studies of child language development*. New York: Holt, Rinehart & Winston, 1973. Pp.91-127.

Siegel, S. *Nonparametric statistics for the behavioral sciences*. New York: McGraw-Hill, 1956.

Sinclair, H. Developmental psycholinguistics. In J.H. Flavell & D. Elkind (Eds.), *Studies in cognitive development*. New York: Oxford University Press, 1969. Pp.315-336.

Sinclair, H. The role of cognitive structures in language acquisition. In
E.H. Lenneberg & E. Lenneberg (Eds.), *Foundations of language development,
Volume 1*. New York: Academic Press, 1975. Pp.223-238.

Sinclair, H. Conceptualization and awareness in Piaget's theory and its rele-
vance to the child's conception of language. In A. Sinclair, R.J. Jarvella,
& W.J.M. Levelt (Eds.), *The child's conception of language*. Berlin: Springer-Verlag, 1978. Pp.191-200.

Sinclair, H., & Bronckart, J.P. S.V.O. A linguistic universal? A study in developmental psycholinguistics. *Journal of Experimental Child Psychology*,
1972, 14, 329-348.

Slobin, D.I. Cognitive prerequisites for the development of grammar. In C.A.
Ferguson & D.I. Slobin (Eds.), *Studies of child language development*.
New York: Holt, Rinehart & Winston, 1973. Pp.175-208.

Slobin, D.I. A case study of early language awareness. In A. Sinclair, R.J.
Jarvella, & W.J.M. Levelt (Eds.), *The child's conception of language*.
Berlin: Springer-Verlag, 1978. Pp.45-54.

Smith, L.B., & Kemler, D.G. Levels of experienced dimensionality in children
and adults. *Cognitive Psychology*, 1978, 10, 502-532.

Smither, S.J., Smiley, S.S., & Rees, R. The use of perceptual cues for number
judgment by young children. *Child Development*, 1974, 45, 693-699.

Swinney, D.A., & Hakes, D.T. Effects of prior context upon lexical access
during sentence comprehension. *Journal of Verbal Learning and Verbal Behavior*, 1976, 15, 681-690.

Trehub, S.E., & Abramovitch, R. Less is not more: further observations on
nonlinguistic strategies. *Journal of Experimental Child Psychology*, 1978,
25, 160-167.

Treiman, R., & Baron, J. Segmental analysis ability: development and relation
to reading ability. In T.G. Waller & G.E. MacKinnon (Eds.), *Reading research: advances in theory and practice, Volume 2*. New York: Academic Press,
in press.

Trevarthen, C. Descriptive analyses of infant communicative behavior. In H.R.
Schaffer (Ed.), *Studies in mother-infant social interaction*. London:
Academic Press, 1977. Pp.227-270.

Tuddenham, R.D. Theoretical regularities and individual idiosyncrasies. In
D.R. Ross, M.P. Ford, & G.B. Flamer (Eds.), *Measurement and Piaget*. New
York: McGraw-Hill, 1971. Pp.64-75.

Wales, R., & Campbell, R. On the development of comparison and the comparison
of development. In G.B. Flores d'Arcais & W.J.M. Levelt (Eds.), *Advances
in psycholinguistics*. Amsterdam: North-Holland Publishing, 1970. Pp.373-
396.

Weir, R. *Language in the crib*. The Hague: Mouton, 1962.

Wellman, H.M. The development of memory monitoring: the feeling of knowing
experience. Unpublished Ph.D. dissertation, University of Minnesota, 1975.

Winkelmann, W. Factorial analysis of children's conservation task performance.
Child Development, 1974, 45, 843-848.

Winner, E. New names for old things: the emergence of metaphoric language.
Journal of Child Language, 1979, 6, 469-492.

Winner, E., Rosenstiel, A.K., & Gardner, H. The development of metaphoric
understanding. *Developmental Psychology*, 1976, 12, 289-297.

Yussen, S.R., & Bird, E. The development of metacognitive awareness in memory,
communication, and attention. *Journal of Experimentel Child Psychology*,
1979, 28, 300-313.

Zhurova, L.Ye. The development of analysis of words into their sounds by
preschool children. In C.A. Ferguson and D.I. Slobin (Eds.), *Studies of
child language development*. New York: Holt, Rinehart & Winston, 1973.
Pp.141-154.

Zifcak, M. Phonological awareness and reading acquisition in first grade
children. Unpublished Ph.D. dissertation, University of Connecticut, 1978.

Subject Index

Abstract nouns 53-54
Acceptability 21-22,25-28,30,50-57, 73-87,89-95,99,104
Alliteration 34-35
Ambiguity 22,24,30-31,100
Amount, *see* Size and amount
Animate nouns 52,53-54
Anomalous imperatives, *see* Imperatives
Assertion 27-28,55,83-84,85, *see also* Content-oriented responses
Automatic processing 22-24,98
Awareness 23,105

"Before" and "after", *see* Temporal relations sentences

Circle, *see* Norman loop
Cleft sentences 7-8,29-30,43-44,64, 66-67,71-72
Clinical method 57
Cognitive flexibility 38
Comprehension strategies, *see* Heuristic strategies
Comprehension task 49-50,63-64
Concrete nouns 53-54
Concrete operations 2,14-19,36-40, 97-108
Conservation 10-13,18,36,42,61-63, 89-95,98,100-101

Content-oriented responses 28,81-87, 99, *see also* Assertion
Content words 8,25
Controlled processing 22-24,38-39, 97-98,101
Curvature perception, *see* Circle

Décalage 38,39,85
Decentering 14,38,73,98
Deviant sentences, *see* Acceptability

Early childhood 2-3,5-19
Existentials, *see* Locative existential sentences

Figurative language, *see* Metaphor, Simile

Goldschmid-Bentler Concept Assessment Kit 42
Grammar 26,50,77-78,80-82,99
Grammatical constraints 85,91

Heuristic strategies 8-18,26,38,39, 97-98,102

Imperatives 25,26
Inalienable possession 55
Inanimate nouns 52,53-54
Incongruity 30

Indefinites, *see* Indeterminates
Indeterminates   54-55,78
Infants   4-5
Inference   8-18
Infinitival complement construction
    16-17
Intransitive verbs   53

Jokes, *see* Puns, Riddles

Locative existential sentences   44-
    45,66-67,71
Locative prepositions   44
Loop, *see* Möbius strip

Matrix permutation task   36
Meaningful false sentences   55-56,
    73-74,84
Memory   67-73,91,102
Mental representation   23-24,29,36,
    67-73
Metacognitive development   38
Metamemory   38,102-103
Metaphor   35,36,106
Middle childhood   2-3,28-40,97-108
Mnemonic strategies   102
Möbius strip, *see* Curvature percep-
    tion
Mundane cognition   6

Negation   54-55,78
Norman loop, *see* Loop

One-word utterances   4
Opaque language   37,98
Operational reversibility   36
Operativity factor   36

Parallel transmission   33
Passive sentences   7,9,17,29-30,36,
    43-44,64,66-67,71-72
Phoneme monitoring   33
Phonemic segmentation   31-35,36,57,
    87-89,90-95,99
Phonological awareness   31-35,36
Phonological feature matrices   33
Phonological units   31-35
Piaget, Jean   4-5,10,14,38,103-104
Picture selection task   29,48-50
Preoperational period   5-19,97,103
Puns   30-31,34

Reading   36,37
Recall   29, *see also* Memory
Recognition   29
Referent   28,31
Reflected abstraction   38
Response bias   58,76-77
Reversible sentences   29,43-44,72
Rhyme   34-35,100,106
Riddle   30-31, *see also* Ambiguity
Rule violation   50-56

Scalogram analysis   62-63,94-95
Segmentation, *see* Phonemic segmenta-
    tion, Syllabic segmentation
Selectional restriction   52,53-54,
    77-79
Self-embedded sentences   21
Semantic representation   23-24,69-73
Sensory-motor period   4-5
Simile   35,106
Size and amount   47,71
Social development   4
"Some" and "any", *see* Indeterminates
Spatial relations sentences   46-47,
    71

Speech perception 31-34,37
Spoken words 31-35,104, *see also*
 Phonemic segmentation
Strategies, *see* Heuristic strat-
 egies
Subcategorization rules 53,77-79
Syllabic segmentation 31,33,57
Symbolic representation 5
Synonymy 22-24,36-37,42-48,65-73,
 90-95,98
Syntactic development 2,7-14,27
Syntax, *see* Grammar, Grammatical
 constraints

Telegraphic imperatives, *see* Impera-
 tives
Temporal relations sentences 45-46,
 64,66-68,71
Transitive verbs 53
Transparent language 37,98

Vocabulary development 16

Word order 8-9,25-26,27,52,77-79

G. Herdan

The Advanced Theory of Language as Choice and Chance

1966. 30 figures. XVI, 459 pages
(Kommunikation und Kybernetik in
Einzeldarstellungen, Band 4)
ISBN 3-540-03584-2

Contents: Introduction. – Language as
Chance I – Statistical Linguistics. –
Language as Choice I – Stylostatistics. –
Language as Chance II – Optimal Systems
of Language Structure. – Language as
Choice II – Linguistic Duality. – Statistics
for the Language Seminary. – Author
Index. Subject Index.

G. Hammarström

Linguistic Units and Items

1976. 17 figures. IX, 131 pages
(Communication and Cybernetics,
Volume 9)
ISBN 3-540-07241-1

Contents: Introduction. – Spoken
Language. – Written Language. – Written
Language in Relation to Spoken Lang-
uage. – Spoken Language in Relation to
Written Language. – The Tasks of
Linguistics. – Bibliography. – Author
Index. – Subject Index.

Springer-Verlag
Berlin
Heidelberg
New York

H. Hörmann

Psycholinguistics

An Introduction to Research and Theory
Translated from the German edition by H.H. Stern
1971. 69 figures. XII, 377 pages
ISBN 3-540-05159-7

„...provides a comprehensive introduction to the psychology of language by concentrating on the behaviourist conception...
the translation is written in a clear, concise and compact English...
The substance of this book, which has become a standard textbook in German as well as the brilliancy of its translation will certainly secure its position in the English speaking world as well."   *IRAL (Deutschland)*

B. Malmberg

Structural Linguistics and Human Communication

An Introduction into the Mechanism of Language and the Methodology of Linguistics
Reprint of the 2nd revised edition 1967
1976. 88 figures. VIII, 213 pages
(Kommunikation und Kybernetik in Einzeldarstellungen, Band 2)
ISBN 3-540-03888-4

Contents: Introduction. – Signs and Symbols. The Linguistic Sign. – The Communication Process. – Preliminary Expression Analysis. Acoustic and Physiological Variables. Information. – Segmentation. Forms of Expression. Oppositions and Distinctions. – Paradigmatic Structures. – Redundancy and Relevancy. Levels of Abstraction. – The Distinctive Feature Concept. The Binary Choice. – Syntagmatic Structures. Distribution and Probability. – Content Analysis. – The Functions of Language. – Perception and Linguistic Interpretation. – Primitive Structures and Defective Language. – Linguistic Change. – Bibliographical Notes. – Author Index. – Subject Index.

"A general survey of modern structural linguistics by B. Malmberg...
The book is essentially intended for the advanced student, but others will also find it useful, since the author manages to deal lucidly and intelligibly with a difficult subject."   *The Years Work in English Studies*

Springer-Verlag
Berlin
Heidelberg
New York